GREAT DEAF AMERICANS

by
Robert Panara
and
John Panara

Illustrated by
Kevin Mulholland

© Robert Panara, John Panara and Kevin Mulholland

T.J. PUBLISHERS, INC.
817 Silver Spring Avenue, 305-D
Silver Spring, Maryland 20910

Printed in the United States of America. All rights reserved.
ISBN #0-932666-17-5   softbbound
ISBN #0-932666-20-5   hardbound
Library of Congress Catalog No.: 83-050071

To
Shirley Fischer Panara
A
GREAT GIRL FRIDAY!

Preface

Any collection of biographies has to be selective. A single volume, such as this, can only represent a fraction of those deaf persons in America, living or dead, who deserve to be called *great*. That was one of the challenges of writing this book. Deciding who should be included, and why. Obviously, no two readers will agree with our final selections, which number thirty-three. Others may find fault with the title chosen for this book.

What we did was to choose a representative group of deaf Americans, past and present, who would illustrate a variety of career interests and achievements. The pattern of their life should also parallel the experience of countless others who have followed the American dream of fulfillment through opportunity. They would also typify the pioneer spirit by overcoming certain handicaps, by their daring and perseverance, and by contributing to the cultural development of America. Thus, we call them *great* because that is how we regard their individual achievement or success story.

They are presented in chronological order so that readers may trace the progress and the aspirations of the deaf community from its earliest roots to its present day place in the sun. Hence, this representative little melting pot of thirty-three *Great Deaf Americans.*

The Authors

Introduction

As all individuals affiliated with deafness know, this disability, which affects some 16 million persons in the United States today, can be a devastating handicap. It shuts off an individual from the people around him through a breakdown in the communication process. It has been called the "invisible" handicap, and rightfully so, because there are few outward signs of the disability and, because of this, much misunderstanding about deafness remains. Deafness, and the communication difficulties it creates, affects a person's entire being—his family life, education, socialization and employment.

Great Deaf Americans is a timely and welcome book. It comes at a time in our history when deaf people are searching for their own identity and developing pride in their heritage and culture. This book is a collection of success stories about individuals who have had to cope with deafness most of their lives. The production of this book in itself is an interesting success story. Not only is it a book *about* deaf people, but it was almost entirely produced by deaf persons—including one of the authors, the illustrator and the typist—and it is being published by a deaf publisher.

In selecting subjects for this book, the authors encountered a formidable task. Who should they include? Who should they leave out? It was no easy assignment. What they have put together here is an interesting and a representative group of successful deaf persons from different walks of life who have been deafened at varying ages, schooled under different methods and, in spite of some terrific odds, made their mark. These individuals are a credit to all of us. Not only did they turn their deafness into a challenge, but they—and indeed the world in which they live—are better for it.

Challenge is the common thread that runs true throughout each story. Each story illustrates in a different way that deafness need not be a barrier to one's success. This book will appeal to young and old alike, and it will serve as an inspiration especially to younger deaf readers.

These individuals' lives will stand as a model for young deaf students, as did the deaf teachers I had during my school days. In my writing experience three teachers—all deaf—stand out. I am indebted to each, because they stimulated, challenged and inspired me and, most important of all, because each imparted to me his own love for writing. One of them was Prof. Robert F. Panara.

Jack R. Gannon, Director
Alumni/Public Relations
Gallaudet College
Author, DEAF HERITAGE: A Narrative
History of Deaf America (1981)

Acknowledgements

We are indebted to those individuals, publications, and organizations for the background information which helped provide material for this book and which is listed in the *Bibliography* herein.

We also appreciate the letters, interviews and conversations with certain deaf persons featured in this book, such as Frances Woods, Boyce Williams, Art Kruger, Robert Weitbrecht, Donald Ballantyne, Malcolm Norwood, Bernard Bragg, Eugene Hairston, Lowell Myers, William Schyman, Phyllis Frelich, Linda Bove, and Michael Chatoff.

Among others, our special thanks to:

Jack R. Gannon, Director, Office of Alumni and Public Relations, Gallaudet College, Washington, D.C.

Jane A. Kenamore, Archivist of the Rosenberg Library in Galveston, Texas.

Gary S. Messinger of the Advisory Council on Historic Preservation, National Archives, Washington, D.C.

Mary Glenn Hearne of the Public Library of Nashville, Tenn.

The staff of the Wallace Memorial Library, Rochester Institute of Technology, Rochester, N.Y.

The staff of the Gallaudet College Library, Washington, D.C.

The Gallaudet College Alumni Association, Gallaudet College, Washington, D.C.

Stephen W. Koziar of Fulton, Missouri.

Berta Zuther Foster, Secretary of the Christian Mission for the Deaf, Flint, Michigan.

Peter H. Ripley, Superintendent of the Missouri School for the Deaf at Fulton, Missouri.

Billy Bray of "The Wonder Dancers," Youngstown, Ohio.

Mrs. Esther Frelich of Devils Lake, North Dakota.

Mrs. Lee Arnold of Kirkwood, Missouri

Playbill, American Theatre Press, Inc., N.Y.C.

David Hays, Producing Director of the National Theatre of the Deaf, Waterford, Conn.

The Editors of *Ebony Magazine*, Johnson Publishing Co., Chicago, Ill.

The National Association of the Deaf, Silver Spring, Maryland.

T.J. Publishers, Inc., Silver Spring, Maryland.

Dr. Barry Culhane and Prof. Lawrence Mothersell, Department of General Studies, National Technical Institute for the Deaf

Marjorie L. Crum, Media Specialist, and Jere R. Rentzel, Assistant Professor of Printing, National Technical Institute for the Deaf, Rochester, N.Y.

We are especially grateful to Jorge B. Samper, Media Production Specialist at the National Technical Institute for the Deaf, for his technical advice and assistance with the photostat reductions, and to Terrence J. O'Rourke, President of T.J. Publishers, Inc., for his helpful criticism, his confidence and support during the work-in-progress.

Above all, we wish to express our heartfelt gratitude and appreciation to Shirley Fischer Panara for the labor of love which she put into the typing and preparation of the entire manuscript.

The Authors

Contents

America . . . the land of opportunity, whose torch of light and hope is held aloft in the right hand of the Statue of Liberty! A gift from France in 1886, the Statue of Liberty has long been the symbol of opportunity for countless immigrants who have journeyed to America in search of a life of fulfillment. It was most fitting, therefore, that the first deaf person to light the way for other deaf people should come from France. Such was the happy fortune of Laurent Clerc, whose arrival in New York harbor preceded the Statue of Liberty by 70 years!

When Laurent Clerc was born in LaBalme, France, on December 26, 1785, there was cause for much rejoicing in the Clerc household. His father was Mayor of the town and the family could boast of a long line of magistrates in the Clerc lineage. Suddenly, however, misfortune struck. At the age of one, the infant fell from a kitchen chair by accident into a nearby fireplace. He was severely burned on one side of his face and a resulting fever left him totally deaf.

Desperately, his parents tried all kinds of medical advice and treatments in an attempt to cure his deafness. When all efforts failed, it appeared as though young Laurent was destined to spend his life in a "dungeon of darkness," without an education and a means of communication.

Fortunately, he had a sympathetic and devoted uncle, also named Laurent Clerc, who heard about a school for the deaf in Paris. When he was twelve years old, his uncle brought him to Paris and enrolled him in the Royal Institution for the Deaf, where he was placed under the personal tutelage of its Director, the Abbe Roche-Ambroise Sicard.

Sicard's methods of instruction, utilizing sign language and the manual alphabet, brought out the hidden genius in Clerc. The youth completed the course of study in seven years and was rewarded with an appointment as an assistant teacher in the Institution, in charge of the highest class.

In 1816, during his eighth year as a teacher, an event happened which changed the course of his life. He met a young idealist from America, Thomas Hopkins Gallaudet, who had

gone to Paris to learn the best method of educating the deaf. Although Gallaudet could only spend three months at the Royal Institute, he had numerous opportunities to observe the brilliant work of Clerc, whom he called "a master teacher." Gallaudet quickly sized up the situation and his needs. He realized that Clerc had the expertise and "the deaf experience" to help him fulfill his mission of founding the first school for the deaf in America, and he offered Clerc the opportunity to become his assistant.

It was a time of decision. Should he accept it or decline the offer? If he accepted, he would be leaving his homeland, his family and friends, his native language—everything he cherished. It meant going to a strange new world across the seas, learning the English language, working with strangers, and coping with the thousand and one problems of founding a school for the deaf. "The first of its kind in America!" That was the challenge—and the crying need! He could envision the helpless deaf children in America, living out their lives in darkness and ignorance. How similar to his own experience, and how lucky he was to escape that fate by being educated at the Royal Institution for the Deaf in Paris!

Like a true pioneer, Clerc accepted. Permission was granted to him by his mentor, the Abbe Sicard, who also gave him his blessing. Finally, after bidding farewell to his family and relatives, Clerc departed from France with Gallaudet on June 18, 1816, on board the *Mary Augusta*.

The voyage across the Atlantic proved both hazardous and overlong. The ship was often buffeted by strong winds; at other times, it came to a standstill when not even a breeze stirred the sails. Altogether, the crossing lasted 52 days, but Clerc and Gallaudet made good use of this time. Gallaudet taught Clerc the English language and Clerc taught Gallaudet sign language. It was the start of a lasting relationship between these men, the one deaf and the other hearing, in which they would share their knowledge and skills.

They arrived in New York on August 9th, and then journeyed by stagecoach to Hartford where Gallaudet planned to establish the school for the deaf. First, however, it was necessary to influence people and raise the needed funds. With Gallaudet as his interpreter, Clerc gave many speeches and demonstrations of methods of teaching the deaf. Beginning with October, they spent the next seven months traveling throughout the East, from Boston to Philadelphia, during which time they also interviewed parents of deaf children and prospective students.

Finally, their mission was accomplished successfully and the first school was established at Hartford. It opened its doors on April 15, 1817, with Gallaudet as the principal and Clerc as head teacher.

Clerc went on to become the most important influence on the education of the deaf in the first half of the nineteenth century. His career as a teacher in America covered 41 years.

During that time, he also taught sign language to new teachers and trained them in methods of teaching the deaf. As new schools opened up in America, their administrators and teachers came to the Hartford school to receive training in communication and methods of instruction.

His life was made happier by marriage to a former pupil, Elizabeth Broadman, and the four children who added joy to the thriving family. He was also honored in many ways. Excellent portraits of him were painted in oil by the noted American artist, Charles Willson Peale, and by the famed deaf artist, John Carlin. In 1864, he was invited to speak at the first Commencement of the newly-established National Deaf-Mutes College (Gallaudet College) in Washington, D.C. And in recognition of his pioneering achievements, Trinity College and Amherst College awarded him with honorary degrees.

At the age of 84, Laurent Clerc breathed his last on July 18, 1869. Several years afterwards, a dedication ceremony in his memory was held at Hartford by his many friends and admirers. They unveiled a bronze bust of his likeness and the inscription underneath it bore the eulogy:

"The Apostle to the Deaf-Mutes of the New World"

In 1921, the school in downtown Hartford was moved to its present location in suburban West Hartford and renamed The American School for the Deaf. There, the memory of its first deaf teacher was preserved in stone when one of the new buildings was named The Laurent Clerc Residential Hall. His name was further perpetuated in verse by Stephen W. Koziar, a deaf poet and alumnus. Entitled "Laurent Clerc", the following excerpts continue to honor his pioneering spirit:

> "Forsaken of your friends and native land,
> You came to guide our cause—great Servitor!
> And in our deep and dark imprisonment,
> We hailed you, Clerc—a stranger to our shore. . . .

Your heart was steeped in cause of humankind;
You came as one heroic volunteer
To free us from the gall . . . we know full well
How heart of yours came reaching to us here.

You helped us break the fetters of the mind.
You guided us with gestures eloquent
To make us sense and comprehend . . . and, lo,
Our hands became a speaking instrument! . . . .

We welcomed you a stranger when you came
To serve and lead us through the trying tide;
And now we cherish you—and evermore—
O Clerc, our benefactor, friend and guide!"

Another alumnus, Gilbert Eastman, who is Director of the Theatre Department at Gallaudet College, spent several months in France researching material for a full length play, which he completed in 1976. Entitled *Laurent Clerc: A Profile*, Eastman's play dramatizes the turning points in Clerc's life and it was performed by the Gallaudet College players on the occasion of the formal dedication of the Clerc Residence Hall at the American School for the Deaf. Thus, the spirit of Laurent Clerc lives on—in stone and in bronze, in poetry and drama—and, above all, in the expressive language of signs and fingerspelling which he brought over from France and passed on to us, like the torch of learning and opportunity.

Deep in the Texas Panhandle, there is a vast area of land known as "Deaf Smith County." Its mineral rich farmlands grow "Deaf Smith County Wheat" which is processed into a wide variety of natural food products, including "Deaf Smith Peanut Butter." Hundreds of recipes for wholesome and nutritious meals are listed in a national publication called *The Deaf Smith Country Cookbook.*

In 1974, a popular Italian Western was shown in movie theatres through the world, *Deaf Smith and Johnny Ear.* The movie featured international film star, Anthony Quinn, as the legendary spy who became one of the bravest heroes of the Texan Revolution in 1836. A year later, a successful biography was written by Cleborne Huston, entitled, *Deaf Smith: Incredible Texas Spy.*

Incredible as it seems, the subject of all this hero worship was actually deaf. He was christened Erastus Smith on April 19, 1789, at his birthplace in Dutchess County, N.Y. A disease in childhood impaired his hearing and he also developed a lung ailment. Hoping that a change of climate would improve his health, the Smith family migrated to Mississippi when Erastus was eleven years old. Here he became active in outdoor life, helping the family work their farm and spending all his free time at hunting and fishing.

He soon developed a wanderlust for the wide open spaces of nearby Texas. He was often away from home, tracking game and hunting buffalo in the company of his "hearing aid dog." Smith trained the dog not to bark whenever it heard a strange noise or the sound of an animal. It would tug at his master's leg to silently warn him of possible danger.

With the rapid settlement of Texas, Smith's reputation as a scout became widespread and he was often in demand as a land surveyor or hunting guide. It was at this time, in 1821, that Mexico won its independence from Spain, putting all of Texas under the rule of the Mexican government.

The following year, Smith married Guadalupe Ruiz Duran, a widow who had three children by her first marriage. They made their home in San Antonio, where Smith became a Mexican citizen. He quickly absorbed the language and customs of the Mexicans, who called him "el Sordo" (the deaf one). He also became acquainted with Col. Jim Bowie and Col. James Fannin, whose sympathies were leaning toward the Texan struggle for independence, although Smith remained a loyal citizen to Mexico.

When the Texan Revolution started in 1835, Smith was immediately under suspicion by the Mexican army. On October 19th, he returned from a buffalo hunt and found San Antonio surrounded by Mexican soldiers. He was denied entry to visit his wife and children. A second attempt the next day was met by armed horsemen who tried to capture "el Sordo." With both guns blazing, Smith escaped and never stopped riding until he reached the camp of the Texan revolutionists, commanded by Gen. Stephen Austin. When the Mexican army posted a reward for the capture of "el Sordo," Smith made his decision. He enlisted as a volunteer in the army of Gen. Austin.

On his first mission, Smith guided a company commanded by Col. Bowie and Col. Fannin behind the enemy lines. Smith fired the first shot at the Battle of Concepcion on October 27, 1835. The surprise attack, in a thick fog, ended with a smashing victory—only one Texan was killed whereas nearly 100 Mexicans were killed and wounded. Thereafter, "el Sordo" became a key figure in the revolution. His eagle eyes, his complete knowledge of the territory, and his bravery quickly attracted the attention of General Sam Houston, Commander-in-chief of the Texan Army.

When Houston learned about "the sack of the Alamo" by the 3,000 soldiers under General Santa Ana, the Mexican Commander, Smith was sent to the Alamo to get more information, accompanied by his companion scout, Capt. Johnny "Ear" Karnes. They returned with the only three survivors of the Alamo—a woman, her fifteen-month-old baby, and a black servant.

Houston rewarded the deaf scout by putting him in command of his own company. So great was Houston's admiration that he never referred to his favorite spy as "Deaf Smith" but always as "the wonderful Mr. E.—the eyes of the Army!"

The turning point of the revolution for the independence of Texas occurred on April 21, 1836, at the Battle of San Jacinto. It took place at Vince's Bayou, where Santa Ana had amassed a large army which outnumbered the Texas force. Heavy rains had flooded the surrounding embankments and Santa Ana's armies had used the only bridge to cross the San Jacinto River, named "Vince's Bridge."

The deaf spy quickly sized up the situation and proposed a daring stratagem to his general. If the Texans staged a surprise offensive, he could destroy the bridge with a band of volunteers. The enemy would then be trapped, without a means of retreat.

Wasting no time, Houston agreed to the plan. Their timing was perfect as they attacked while the Mexican soldiers were asleep during the noontime hours of siesta. Simultaneously, the Texan volunteers led by Deaf Smith cut down "Vince's Bridge" with their axes.

So sudden and so devastating was the Texan offensive that the battle lasted less than an hour. One of the most active participants in the heavy fighting was Deaf Smith, who held his axe high overhead as he opened the enemy ranks, shouting in his high-pitched squeaky voice, "The bridge is down! They can't get away, men! Remember the Alamo!"

The revolution came to a victorious end the next day with the capture of Santa Ana. At this historic event, Smith was given an honored place in the very front row of all the military dignitaries, right next to Gen. Houston. The scene was later reproduced in a huge painting by William H. Huddle. It depicts Gen. Houston, wounded in battle, lying on a blanket as he accepts the surrender of Santa Ana. Seated at his side is Deaf Smith, who cups his ear to hear, if he can, the terms of unconditional surrender.

As a reward for his heroic deeds, Smith was made a captain in command of a company of Texas rangers. After one year, however, he retired. A war wound, and the recurrence of the lung ailment that plagued his childhood, finally took its toll. His death came at the age of fifty, on November 30, 1837. It is said that no member of his family attended the funeral, and he was buried in an unmarked grave.

A man of many talents and interests, John Carlin personified the "Renaissance spirit" of 19th century America. He was an artist and a poet; he wrote about architecture and geology; he promoted the cause of higher education of the deaf and contributed greatly to their welfare; and he knew five foreign languages. What made this all the more remarkable is the fact that he began life as a poor boy who had to leave school at the age of twelve.

John Carlin was born in Philadelphia, Pa., on June 15, 1813. His deafness was congenital, as was the case with his brother Andrew, born three years later. Their father, a poor shoemaker, could not afford to give them a special education—the only two schools for the deaf at that time being in Hartford and New York City. Unable to communicate with anyone, young Carlin took to roaming around the streets of Philadelphia in search of adventure.

These walking tours must have captured the imagination of the little deaf boy and influenced his interest in art and architecture. They made him gaze with delight and wonder at the picturesque old city with all its kingly domes, its soaring pinnacles and church towers, its beautiful parks and landscapes.

He first tried his hand as an artist by drawing chalk figures and fantastic shapes on the kitchen floor at home. His mother, however, could not appreciate such "masterpieces," which were quickly erased by her floor mop. Fortunately, there was a "guardian angel" looking after the little deaf boy.

While roaming the streets one day, Carlin met a kind old gentleman who took him aside and tried to communicate with him. The man was David G. Seixas, a Jewish crockery merchant with a special interest in the welfare and education of needy deaf children whom he found wandering the streets of Philadelphia. Seixas gave them food and clothing, and he had also set up a private school in his home, where he taught them "the three R's" by method of a self-invented sign language.

Although Carlin was six years old at that time and didn't know a word of English, he was to become the brightest star in that one-room school which enrolled 15 children of different ages. He could also thank his lucky stars that, in the following year, the state assumed the responsibility of running Mr. Seixas' school. It also added several experienced teachers of the deaf to the staff.

One of these was Laurent Clerc, the brilliant deaf teacher from the Hartford School who was on loan as a visiting educator to help the new school get started. Although Clerc stayed for only one year, his influence was widespread—and it touched John Carlin. The School, later to become the Mt. Airy School for the Deaf, was successfully launched, and John Carlin discovered a brave new world of knowledge in his books. He also showed a special talent for painting.

He pursued these two interests, reading and painting, with such intensity that he was graduated in 1925 at the age of twelve. Thereafter, he supported himself by working as a sign and house painter by day. At night, he studied by candlelight. By the age of 19, he not only had a solid background in art history but he also mastered English and 5 different foreign languages. He chose these subjects because he was determined to someday go to Europe to study art.

He first went to New York City with his hard-earned savings to study drawing under J. R. Smith and portrait painting under John Neagle. The experience proved he had real talent, and Carlin was convinced that he should go to Europe for advanced study.

First, however, he had to return to the business of house painting and save enough money. This he did, by 1838, when he went to London to study at the British Museum. He then went to France, where he took lessons in portrait painting under the famous teacher, Paul Delaroche. Carlin knew the French language so well that he progressed rapidly in his studies. He also used pad and pencil to interpret the lessons for another American student—a hearing man who didn't know French!

In 1841, Carlin returned to America and began working as

a painter of miniature portraits in New York City, where he set up his studio. Among his patrons were various members of the Knickerbocker families of "Old Amsterdam." It was the beginning of many contacts that Carlin would make with prominent persons in society.

In 1843, Carlin married Constance Wayland, who had attended the New York Institution for the Deaf. Miss Wayland was the niece of the Hon. William H. Seward, Governor of New York, who later became U.S. Senator and Secretary of State under Pres. Abraham Lincoln.

Carlin was a gifted artist whose specialty was in painting miniature portraits on ivory. Soon, his work became greatly in demand and many famous people asked him to paint their portrait. These patrons included Senator Seward, Hamilton Fish, Thurlow Weed, Horace Greeley and Jefferson Davis who was Secretary of War under President Franklin Pierce.

When photography became popular and there was less demand for miniature portrait painting, Carlin changed over to do landscape and genre painting. He produced many outstanding oil paintings, some of them later displayed at the Detroit Institute of Arts and in the International Art Exhibit of Deaf Painters at New York, 1935.

By this time, Carlin's success as an artist became so profitable that he was able to give more time to other interests. One of these was writing poetry. For many years, he had experimented with poetic expression, and finally he learned to compose poems in perfect rhythm and rhyme. Some of his poems were printed in leading newspapers and he was commended for his work by William Cullen Bryant, the poet and Editor of the *New York Post.* In commenting on this achievement, Dr. Edward M. Gallaudet, President of Gallaudet College, said "We should as well expect a man born blind to paint a picture as a congenitally deaf man to write a poem" ("Poetry of the Deaf," *Harpers Monthly*, March, 1884).

Carlin's other writings covered a wide range of topics. *The Philadelphia Courier* featured several of his articles on archi-

LAURENT CLERC
1785 - 1869
AMERICA'S FIRST DEAF TEACHER
PAINTING BY JOHN CARLIN
PRESENTED TO:
KENTUCKY SCHOOL FOR THE DEAF
DANVILLE, KENTUCKY

tecture. He wrote a book for children, *The Scratchsides Family.* His writings frequently appeared in publications of the deaf on subjects ranging from "geology," "great books," and "methods of educating the deaf."

Like the hero in the *Horatio Alger* stories, Carlin was a self-educated person who rose from "rags to riches." However, he knew the value of higher education for the deaf. Largely through his influence and example, Edward M. Gallaudet was inspired to establish the world's only college for the deaf. At its first Commencement Day in 1865, Carlin was the first person to be awarded an honorary degree. He also gave the Commencement Address in eloquent sign language, in which he predicted the future greatness of Gallaudet College and the promise of better career opportunities for its deaf graduates.

It is significant, too, that Carlin was inspired to paint the best likeness of Laurent Clerc, the deaf teacher who helped shape his destiny. This oil portrait still hangs in a conspicuous place in the Kentucky School for the Deaf.

The deaf community is also indebted to John Carlin for his many contributions to their welfare. He led the movement to erect a monument in memory of Thomas Hopkins Gallaudet in Hartford, Conn. For this, he designed a side panel which portrays Gallaudet teaching his first pupils. He helped raise the sum of $6,000 to build St. Ann's Episcopal Church for the Deaf in New York City, and he headed the committee that raised a building fund for the Gallaudet Home for the Aged and Infirm Deaf. And he was one of the first to encourage the cultural progress of the deaf by founding the Manhattan Literary Association of the Deaf.

When John Carlin died on April 23, 1891, the entire deaf community could sense that there had passed away "a glory and a greatness from the earth." A brilliant thinker and a man of many skills, he could well be called "the Leonardo da Vinci of the deaf" and the very model of a "Renaissance man."

During the Civil War, a young correspondent was sent to Washington, D.C., to cover the news for the *St. Louis Republican* newspaper. The writer of these war dispatches was "Howard Glyndon," who also wrote feature articles based on interviews with important persons in the government and military. Few readers of the *St. Louis Republican* knew that "Howard Glyndon" was a *woman*, and none knew that she was *totally deaf!* Her name was Laura Redden—the first deaf "libber" in America, and the first to succeed in the field of journalism and literature.

Laura Redden was born on February 9, 1840, in Somerset County, Maryland. After her family had moved to St. Louis, Mo., she became totally deaf at the age of 10 from an attack of spinal meningitis which also impaired her speech. This made her develop the habit of writing when she communicated with people, and "pad and pencil" became her constant companions wherever she went.

After completing her education at the Missouri School for the Deaf, Laura Redden became an assistant editor in 1859 for *The Presbyterian and Our Union,* a religious newspaper published in St. Louis. In 1860, she began contributing poems and articles for the *St. Louis Republican.* When the Civil War began, she was looked upon as a "literary patriot" who strongly supported the Union cause, and the *Republican* sent her to Washington to keep up with the latest news about the war.

This talented and lively woman from the "Show Me" state of Missouri soon began a long and successful career as a journalist, biographer, and poet. Among the famous men she met and interviewed were President Lincoln, General Grant, and General Garfield. She published a book of mini-biographies, *Notable Men in the House of Representatives* (1862), which was greatly admired for its fine writing and vivid portrayal of personalities. In 1865, she published her collection of poems about the Civil War, *Idylls of Battle and Poems of the Rebellion.* One of these poems, "Belle Missouri," became the favorite song or "battle cry" of the Union soldiers from Missouri.

When the war ended, Redden went to Europe where she learned French, German, Italian and Spanish. She continued writing for the *Republican* and also wrote for two New York newspapers, *The Sun* and *The Times.* Her articles, expressed in an easy, informal style, covered such topics as People, Places, Politics, and Books.

She returned to the U.S. in 1868 and joined the staff of the *New York Evening Mail.* Making her home in New York City, she also contributed many poems for popular magazines such as *Harper's, The Atlantic Monthly, Putnam's,* and *Galaxy.* Her second book of poems, *Sounds From Secret Chambers,* was published in 1874.

In an attempt to improve her speech and lipreading, she went to the Clarke School for the Deaf at Northampton, Mass., for two years. She also studied speech and lipreading under Prof. Alexander Graham Bell in nearby Boston, and the result was that she developed a clear and pleasant speaking voice. However, she never mastered lipreading and continued to communicate with people, as well as do newspaper interviews, by method of pad and pencil.

In 1876, she married Edward W. Searing, a successful New York lawyer. They had one child, a daughter. The family then moved to California in 1886 when Laura Searing's health began to fail. One of her last poems, "The Hills of Santa Cruz," expressed her feelings for the beautiful place she called her home, as illustrated by the following excerpts:

> "I've seen the far-off Apennines
>   Melt into dreamy skies;
> I've seen the peaks the Switzers love
>   In snowy grandeur rise;
> And many more, to which the world
>   Its praise cannot refuse—
> But of them all, I love the best
>   The hills of Santa Cruz!
>
> Oh, how serenely grand they stand,
>   Beneath the morning sun!
> Oh, how divinely fair they are
>   When morn to noon hath run!
> How virginal their fastnesses,
>   Where no Bacchante woos
> The kisses of the grapes that grow
>   On the hills of Santa Cruz! . . . ."

This poem greatly impressed the noted American poet, John Greenleaf Whittier, who said that "it would cling to the Santa Cruz mountains forever" and immortalize the picturesque seaside village the same way as Bret Harte's writings did for San Francisco.

Obviously, she fell in love with her adopted state of California. A few years later, she sang in praise of it again in her poem, "The Unveiling of the Fountain," which also honored the famous deaf sculptor, Douglas Tilden. This occurred in San Francisco on September 5, 1897 at the unveiling of Tilden's statue, *Admission Day*, which commemorated California's admission into the United States in 1850.

After 1908, her pen ceased to be productive. Her last years were spent as a semi-invalid living with her daughter in San Mateo. In 1921, her daughter published a collection of her mother's poems, *Echoes of Other Days.*

Laura Redden Searing died on August 10, 1923. Her achievement as a poet and journalist was recognized by her peers in the literary world. She was included in the *Dictionary of American Biography* (1928), and her poems were featured in several anthologies of American literature, edited by such popular poets as John Greenleaf Whittier and William Cullen Bryant.

Almost everybody knows about the story of Alexander Graham Bell and his invention of the telephone. Not many are aware, however, that he was also a teacher of the deaf and that he married one of his students. Her name was Mabel Hubbard, and the story of her life is just as inspiring as that of her famous husband.

Mabel Hubbard was born on November 25, 1857 in Cambridge, Massachusetts. At the age of five, she developed scarlet fever which caused total deafness. When it was discovered that Mabel still had some ability to speak, her parents were determined to have her associate with their hearing daughters at home rather than send her away to a school for the deaf for her education. Fortunately, they met young Mary True while vacationing in Maine and engaged her to become the governness of their four school age daughters.

Although Mary True had never met a deaf child before, she was a "born teacher." Little Mabel quickly learned her "3R's" at home, and this opportunity to share learning experiences and everyday activities with her hearing sisters influenced her whole life. She became outgoing, comfortable in the company of hearing persons, and a talented lipreader.

At the age of nine, Mabel was given an examination by a teacher from the Boston public schools that proved she compared favorably with hearing children of her age, and even older. This achievement encouraged her father, Gardner Hubbard, to petition the Governor for the establishment of a school in Massachusetts where deaf children could be educated by means of the oral method.

Young Mabel played a dramatic role when the legislative committee met to vote on the petition. As the "star witness," she charmed the committee by her poise and intelligence in answering questions. Although her speech was not normal, they clearly understood her and they marveled at how skillfully she read their lips—even those gentlemen with full beards! Their favorable decision led to the founding of the John Clarke Institution for the Deaf in Northampton, with Gardner Hubbard as president.

It was at this school and in Boston University that Alexander Graham Bell, a young immigrant from Scotland, began his career as a speech therapist and Professor of "Visible Speech," or a graphic method for improving the speech of deaf persons. Mabel Hubbard was sixteen when she entered his class as a pupil in Boston University, and this meeting changed the course of their lives.

At about the same time, Bell had begun experimenting with acoustics and multiple telegraphy, believing that human speech could be carried by telegraph. He also tried to invent an instrument which would transcribe human speech into written symbols or words for the deaf to read and understand. During this period, Bell was in love with Mabel Hubbard, and he worked and dreamed as one inspired.

One day, he was astonished to learn that Mabel's father, a prominent attorney, had a special interest in improving the telegraph system in America. Gardner Hubbard became one of Bell's sponsors and helped him win exclusive rights to the patent after the invention of the telephone. Sixteen months later, Mabel Hubbard agreed to Bell's proposal (made a year earlier) and they were married on July 11, 1877.

With the success of the telephone, Bell became internationally famous. He received countless invitations to give demonstrations and lectures in America and abroad, meeting people from all walks of life and society. Mabel Bell not only kept pace with this busy schedule but she also won admiration as the perfect guest and hostess. These social activities ranged from the most formal receptions in high society to plain old fashioned dinners—in Boston, New York, Washington, D.C., and Baddeck, Nova Scotia.

She loved people; she took a special delight in entertaining them at home; and she knew how important these contacts were to her famous husband. Indeed, it was Mabel who helped Bell overcome his natural shyness and kept him from retreat-

ciation in Nova Scotia, now known as "Canadians Home and School." For her outstanding work, she was made honorary president of the Young Ladies Club, and the townspeople of Baddeck went even further. They passed an ordinance which gave her the right to a Canadian vote—making her the only alien ever to receive this privilege.

Of the four children born to Mabel and Alexander Bell, two survived. They were Elsie and Daisy Bell, who grew up to share their parents' many interests. But nothing gave their parents more joy than when Elsie and Daisy married prosperously and had children of their own. Ma and Pa Bell lived to see seven grandchildren surround them whenever they got together with the Grosvenor and Fairchild families.

The love affair of Mabel and Alexander Bell lasted for a lifetime during which they lived a rich, full life. When Bell passed away at the age of seventy-five, Mabel was heartbroken and desolate. She made a heroic effort to collect her husband's memoirs for a future biographer, and also insure that some of his scientific experiments would be continued, especially those involving the development of hydrofoil boats and sheep breeding. However, her grief was so deep that her heart gave out on January 3, 1923, five months after the death of her beloved husband. She was buried beside him in the grave at "Beinn Bhreagh" ("Beautiful Mountain"), their idyllic summer retreat in Baddeck, Nova Scotia.

It was a story book ending to a story book romance—the kind that also makes the ideal script for a Hollywood movie. And this is how the world remembers them. The romance of Mabel Hubbard and Alexander Graham Bell lives on in the inspiring biography, *Make A Joyful Sound,* by Helen Elmira White. And their love story continues to charm each new generation since 1939 through the motion picture, *The Story of Alexander Graham Bell.* As dramatized by Don Ameche and Loretta Young, it gives us an unforgettable picture of how this vivacious and talented deaf woman won the heart of the great inventor and teacher of the deaf.

ing into his shell of solitude (as was his habit in pursuing many scientific interests and schemes for new inventions).

Mabel was just as interested in new ideas and could also be creative. She wrote a brilliant article, "On the Subtile Art of Lipreading" which appeared in *The Atlantic Monthly* (1895) and was later translated and published in fourteen foreign countries. This article greatly influenced the work of Edward B. Nitchie, the deaf man who established the Nitchie School of Lipreading and whose textbook was dedicated to Mabel Hubbard. She also helped him start the New York League for the Hard of Hearing which provided free lessons in lipreading for persons with hearing impairment.

At their Canadian homestead in Baddeck, Nova Scotia, Mabel conceived and founded "The Young Ladies Club," which was the first women's club in Canada. Later, she used the "Ladies Club" to lobby successfully for the first Parent-Teacher Asso-

Douglas Tilden, a deaf sculptor, produced a number of remarkable works of art during his equally remarkable lifetime. He has been called "genius" and "mastercraftsman" by all who have marveled at the beauty and realism of his statues. "Breathtaking" is how most people describe his work. And this seems interesting, because the very thing that takes an onlooker's breath away is the amazing talent Tilden had for breathing life *into* his chiseled forms. Many of his masterpieces decorate numerous locations in California, his home state, which explains why he has been called "The Michelangelo of the West."

His indestructable statue, *Memorial to Mechanics,* is one of his most famous creations. Located at the intersection of Battery and Market Streets in San Francisco, the huge bronze statue portrays a group of muscular workers as they sweat and toil in an iron foundry. Some people, upon viewing the awe-

some monument, have said that they could almost see the figures come alive. Such enthusiasm should not appear too far-fetched, for there does indeed seem to be something special about the statue. Even the killer earthquake which demolished most of San Francisco in 1906 couldn't destroy it. As the city lay in ruins, there stood the *Mechanics,* alone and unharmed—bronze survivors of a crumbled metropolis!

Douglas Tilden was born in Chico, California, on May 1, 1860 and became deaf when he was 5 years old. After graduating from the State School for the Deaf at Berkeley, he attended the University of California for one year, but left to go back to Berkeley to teach. He became interested in sculpturing in 1883 and practiced for four years during his free time. By 1887, however, his interest had grown into a fascination, and so the young deaf teacher resigned from Berkeley to devote his full attention to the profession of sculpturing. After getting a loan from the State School, Tilden set out for New York where he studied for eight months before deciding to sail for Paris—the capital of the art world, where artisans from all over the globe gathered.

In 1889, while in Paris, Tilden submitted his creation, *Baseball Player,* to the famous Salon des Artistes. The Salon was the same place where Auguste Rodin, the creator of the famous statue *The Thinker,* had first gained recognition, the place that helped transform him almost overnight from an unknown artist to a master. To have an entry approved for exhibit at the Salon was a major accomplishment. Tilden's *Baseball Player* was accepted, and like Rodin, he enjoyed almost instant popularity as a gifted sculptor. The statue is now located at Golden Gate Park, San Francisco, the scene of two other masterworks by him—*Father Junipero Serra* and *California Volunteers.*

Following the success of his *Baseball Player,* Tilden was inspired to create another life-sized figure of a male athlete. Entitled *The Tired Boxer,* it was exhibited at the Salon in 1890 and received Honorable Mention. This was quite an achievement at that time. Only one other American sculptor, Augus-

tus Saint Gaudens, had ever won a similar honor from the famed Salon.

Tilden spent six years in Paris before returning home to California because of dwindling finances. While in Paris, he created his *Bear Hunt* statue which was exhibited at the Salon and later at the Chicago World's Fair in 1893. Standing 9 feet high and 5 feet across, *The Bear Hunt* depicts an American Indian, with upraised tomahawk, caught in the clutches of a giant grizzly bear. This magnificent monument in bronze is now located at the California School for the Deaf at Fremont.

Tilden did more than dramatize the vigor and variety of "the American experience" in his sculptures. He was proud of his native roots, and his chisel often gave expression in stone to the men and events that contributed to the development of California. Among these, the following are still admired today in various locations along the west coast:

> *Father Junipero Serra* (9½ ft. tall) who founded San Francisco and established the long chain of Catholic missions in California.
>
> *Senator Stephen M. White*—the larger than life-size representation of the noted U.S. Senator from California, situated in front of the Los Angeles Law Library.
>
> *California Volunteers*—an imposing monument, 12 ft. in height, which depicts a soldier of the Spanish-American War fighting alongside "Bellona," the goddess of war, who rides the winged horse, Pegasus. Situated in downtown San Francisco.
>
> *Admission Day*—the over-life-size figure of a flag-waving "Forty-niner," which commemorates California's admission into the United States September 9, 1850.

This memorial monument, which also has a fountain at the base, was dedicated on September 5, 1897. It is also fitting that a deaf poet, Laura Redden Searing, composed a poem for the occasion. Titled "The Unveiling of the Fountain," her poem celebrates both the creation and the creator:

"This delicate shaft, so slender, yet so strong
  How proudly it upbears
Its graceful burden, perfect as a song,
  The which it crown-like wears! . . .

For it shall be the joy of him who stands
  All rugged at thy feet
To bear aloft the flag within his hands
  Each nook of earth to greet. . . .

Thy inspirer and thy maker, worthy-each,
  The soil from which they sprung—
For brother-love and love of art they teach;
  Pioneers, though so young. . . .

Oh, California, fair as any dream!
  On thee, the world shall wait;
And steadily the nations all shall stream
  Through the wide Golden Gate!"

Soaring 35 feet into the air, this inspiring monument has now become a landmark attraction in downtown San Francisco.

No wonder that his contemporaries called him "The Michelangelo of the West!" As California's greatest sculptor, Tilden was also honored in 1914 when the Native Sons of the Golden West dedicated their "Hall of Fame" and included him among the 13 native-born Californians who had earned an international reputation in the arts and sciences.

Like many other artists, Tilden experienced both good and hard times. During the good years, he enjoyed the life of an internationally acclaimed artist. He belonged to exclusive groups like the "Bohemian Club" and associated with poets, artists, and writers—among them the novelist, Jack London, the actress, Mary Anderson, and playwright David Belasco. One of his greatest admirers was James D. Phelan, the wealthy United States senator of California, who also sponsored some of Tilden's statues. One of these, *The Football Players*, graces the campus of the University of California in Berkeley.

The years following the turn of the century brought new concerns for the American public. Growing interest in technology and fear of war caused a decline in art appreciation, which in turn, caused difficult times for Tilden. For a while, he was forced to accept state aid. But Tilden's love of art and his desire to help the deaf never stopped. He was a true deaf activist, writing numerous articles on deaf awareness, art and the deaf, and methods for educating deaf children.

On August 6, 1935, Douglas Tilden was found dead in his studio—a victim of a fatal heart attack. An unfinished clay model that he had been working on lay next to him. When informed of his death, artists and admirers around the world mourned the loss of such a great man. But Tilden lives on in his immortal creations which continue to inspire and amaze all who see them. In 1980, his greatness was crowned in glory by Mildred Albronda with the publication of her illuminating biography, *Douglas Tilden: Portrait of a Deaf Sculptor.*

It was a sunny May afternoon in Savannah, Georgia. The year was 1944 and a crowd had gathered at a pier to witness a special event—the launching of a liberty ship, the S.S. *Juliette Low*. After the traditional bottle-breaking on the hull, the ship moved out into the water, looking proud as it cut through the small waves. It was a vessel with a mission: to bring supplies to American troops overseas.

For one year, the S.S. *Juliette Low* journeyed back and forth across the Atlantic, miraculously avoiding enemy submarines which had destroyed hundreds of ships. After awhile, word spread among the sailors that the S.S. *Juliette Low* was under a talisman, that it was a charmed boat.

When the war ended and rumors flew that all liberty ships would be scrapped, the men who had served on the *Low* rallied in protest, exclaiming, "She must be saved!" Their efforts proved successful. Once again the ship escaped destruction, and was used to bring food and clothing to needy people everywhere. During peacetime, the vessel continued to avoid misfortune, weathering storms that had plunged other ships to the bottom of the sea. At each foreign port where the S.S. *Juliette Low* anchored, members of the Girl Scouts or Girl Guides from that country came to greet the good-will ship. Then the captain, if he could speak the language, would tell them the story of the woman—a deaf woman—for whom the ship was named. She was Juliette Gordon Low, founder of the Girl Scouts of America, a woman whose compassion, community spirit, and determination were reflected in the ship that bore her name.

The Girl Scouts of America—with a membership of over three million—is a widely-known and highly respected organization. Yet, few people know who founded it. Even fewer know that its founder was deaf.

Juliette Gordon Low became almost totally deaf in her late twenties. She organized the first Girl Scout troops in America in her hometown, Savannah, in 1912. She was 51 years old at the time. A few other women across the country had started troops of their own around the same time, but Juliette Low is recognized as the founder of the national organization, for it was she who solidified and fostered the movement by providing the necessary funds and leadership. Her interest began in England, where she lived part of her life before 1912. It was there that she began organizing "Girl Guides" troops after meeting Sir Robert Baden-Powell, the founder of the Boy Scouts.

The story of Juliette Low is a remarkable one. She was a poor Southern girl who was educated at "finishing schools," and who later climbed into the ranks of the English elite. Yet, she never failed to acknowledge her sisterhood with the poorest members of society. She was a woman with hundreds of friends, but for every acquaintance from the upper class, there were ten less fortunate who also called her "friend." Her formal training, along with her romantic and spirited temperament, produced an independent and resourceful woman who could get things done regardless of limitations. Her major achievements were accomplished after she became deaf.

Juliette Low's life was as dramatic as the period in which she was born. She entered the world on October 31, 1860, less than a year before the Civil War would begin, at a time when the North and South were already drawing battlelines. The second of six children born to William and Nellie Gordon, young "Daisy" (as she was affectionately called) was a precocious child—quick, witty, and artistic. Her younger years were filled with fear while her father fought for the Southern army. When it became apparent that a Northern victory was inevitable, the family went to Chicago as Union troops poured into Savannah. While in Chicago, Daisy became deathly ill with "brain fever." She recovered fully, but it is possible that the sickness was partly responsible for the deafness she would experience later.

After the war ended and her father returned unharmed, the family moved back to Savannah. The scars of battle were everywhere. Mr. Gordon tried as best as he could to pick up the pieces of his cotton business, but the next few years were spent in poverty. The tragedy that the war brought, however, did not dampen young Juliette's spirits. She waited in anticipation for something to happen.

As the years rolled by, the Gordon's financial situation improved and, at the age of thirteen, Juliette was sent to a boarding school in Virginia. Two years were spent at the Stuart Hall school before Daisy went to the Edge Hill Academy, also in Virginia. At both schools, her zest and free spirit didn't suit the instructors well. Daisy was constantly getting into trouble and receiving demerits for disobeying rules. The infractions were always minor—telling ghost stories to the other girls late at night, or drawing pictures during class. To show her dismay, she invented her own name for the school: "Edge of Hell."

At the age of 16, she went to the Mesdemoiselles Charbonnier's School in New York where the routine was even more disciplined. It was run by two Frenchwomen and students were drilled in decorum and manners. This time, however, Juliette fared better and was put on the "honors" list.

After graduating from the Charbonnier's School, she returned home to Savannah, a young and refined lady. Again, she waited for something to happen. Eventually, she met William Low, the son of a wealthy family from England. The family owned a home in Savannah, and William had been sent to manage the cotton business there. Juliette and William soon fell in love.

It seemed to Juliette, the way things were going, that life was a bouquet of roses. She toured England and met William's parents. But the first thorn eventually appeared. She began experiencing pain in one ear when she was twenty-one and sought relief from a Savannah doctor. The doctor said there was little he could do, but Juliette was stubborn, asking him to inject silver nitrate into her ear. It was a form of treatment she had heard about in New York. Not knowing the proper dosage, the doctor was reluctant, but eventually he agreed to Juliette's demands. Unfortunately, the amount injected was indeed too much and caused a permanent partial loss of hearing in the ear. The partial loss became total a few years later, in 1886, when she married William Low. At the wedding, a grain of rice lodged in the ear causing an infection. Eventually, the other ear was also affected, resulting in a progressive loss of hearing in that ear.

The following summer, the newlyweds moved to England so that William could assist his father in business matters there. The years of training at the schools in Virginia and New York proved their worth more than ever. It was the height of the Victorian period, a time of manners and decorum, when everyone who was anyone drank their tea with the "pinky finger" sticking out. There were hunting meets and costume parties with aristocracy. The image of Juliette Low in those days was that of an elegant lady who took walks through the Wellesbourne countryside with a pair of well-groomed dogs at her heels. Although her deafness grew worse, Low was never cut off from conversation because she usually did all the talking!

Her experiences with the English elite, however, didn't separate her from the common folk. The years spent in poverty had entwined her roots with theirs, establishing empathy. When a woman in town developed what appeared to be leprosy and was shunned by everyone, Low fearlessly visited her, bringing food and chatting for hours. She made regular stops at the workhouse at Stratford-on-Avon to talk to the elderly poor there. When the Spanish-American War broke out in 1898, Low returned to America and worked at a military hospital in Miami.

After the war, she returned home. A few years later, in 1905, her husband died of a debilitating illness. They had been married 19 years.

There had been no children. Alone and isolated by a barrier of silence now almost total, Juliette traveled often to escape the loneliness. She toured Europe, went to India, and of course, made an occasional stop in Savannah. Yet, during the years of world-wide travel, Juliette Low was like a ship without a rudder, drifting aimlessly and without direction. Again, she was waiting for something to happen, something that would give her life meaning.

Her search ended in 1911 when, while staying in Scotland, she met Sir Robert Baden-Powell. Baden-Powell had founded the Boy Scouts in 1908 as a means of teaching self-reliance and resourcefulness to young men. The movement had become very successful and, interestingly enough, over six thousand girls had tried to register. To accommodate them, Baden-Powell enlisted the help of his sister who formed the "Girl Guides." Inspired by the idea, Low decided to try and start her own Girl Guide troop in Scotland. She pictured the many poor girls in the Glen Lyon village who spent most of their days being bored. Within no time, Juliette had formed a Girl Guide troop of seven members. There were lessons in horticulture, wool-spinning, and cooking with imagination. Low managed to find a shop where hand-woven goods were made and convinced the storekeeper to buy all the wool the girls were spinning.

After returning to her home in England, she began organizing Girl Guide troops in London. The girls, most of whom were from London's lower class, enthusiastically learned handicrafting and began to feel positive about themselves.

For the first time in ages, Juliette Low felt excited again. The Girl Guide movement had delivered her from boredom and gave her life a purpose.

That purpose became even more clearly defined when she realized that American girls could benefit just as much from Girl Guiding. In January, 1912, after making sure that her Scottish and English troops were in good hands, Juliette began another journey, to her hometown. Within three months and less than a year after meeting Baden-Powell, two Savannah Girl Guide troops were established. Soon there were six troops and Low was off again to London to learn more about running a national organization. Having learned what she needed to know, she went back to Savannah and began writing letters to the many important friends she had made during her life, friends who could help with a national association.

She re-wrote the English Girl Guide Handbook, adapting it for American girls. Its title was "How Girls Can Help Their Country." The funding for the publication, as well as everything else related to Girl Guiding, came from her own pocketbook. As her financial resources grew thin, she sold her jewelry in order to produce the necessary funding.

Low's life became busier than ever. There were letters to write, people to see, places to go. She went to the White House to speak to interested individuals there. The new image she began to project was that of a politician campaigning across the country. Making full use of her deafness, she refused to take "No" in answer to her requests for help! Soon a little office in Washington, D.C., became the national headquarters. The name was changed to "Girl Scouts," although Juliette preferred the old title.

Girl Scouting was not much different from the Boy Scouts. Besides cooking and handicrafting, girls hiked, played sports, camped, and did many activities considered "unfeminine" at the time. Yet, because the founder and president of the American Girl Scouts was Juliette Low, a fine and well-respected lady, even the most strict parents allowed their daughters to participate in the movement.

Between 1912 and 1917, the proud deaf lady from Savannah traveled back and forth between England and America. The fact that waters were infested with German U-boats did not scare her. Her beloved Girl Guides and Girl Scouts always came first.

In the meantime, troops sprang up in every major city. The national headquarters moved to New York. Growing contributions helped lift some of the financial burden off her shoulders.

In 1919, the International Council of Girl Scouts and Girl Guides was formed and met in London, during which time the founder of the American Girl Scouts proudly announced that membership in the states was at 40,000. After the meeting, Low returned to America. At the National Convention in January, she resigned as president so that she could devote more time to international matters, seeking to bring Girl Scouting and Guiding organizations in every country together.

International Conferences, or "World Camps," met every two years starting in 1920. At each, Juliette Low represented the United States. The 1920, '22, and '24 Conferences were held in England. None were scheduled for America until 1928. Low's dream was to have the 1926 meeting in the U.S. instead of in Switzerland, as had been planned. To her, it seemed only right that the U.S. be next in line to host a convention. In a show of respect and tribute to the woman who had been the guiding light of the movement in America, the executive board voted to hold the 1926 World Camp in the states. It was a proud moment for Low as four hundred American Girl Scout leaders and over 50 representatives from twenty-nine foreign countries paraded up New York City's Fifth Avenue and then proceeded to Camp Macy on the Hudson for the convention.

It was indeed fitting that the 1926 World Camp was held in America, for Juliette Low would not live to see the 1928 Convention.

Since 1923, she hid the fact that she was fighting cancer. Her health had always been bad, but there never was much time, especially during the Girl Scout movement, to think about it. When Juliette had the time, she visited specialists, but nothing could be done about the cancer. She died on January 17, 1927 in her hometown. The Girl Scouts of America numbered 167,000 members then. Fifty years later it had over 3,000,000.

During the last weeks of her life, messages of appreciation poured in from all over the world. Her favorite one was a telegram from the Girl Scout National Council. The message read: "You are not only the first Girl Scout, but the best Girl Scout of them all."

Juliette Low was buried in Laurel Grove Cemetary, Savannah, dressed in her Girl Scout uniform.

The telegram that she loved so much was folded and tucked away in her pocket.

CINCINNATI

"Take me out to the ball game . . .
If we don't win it's a shame,
For it's *one, two, three strikes and you're out*
In the old ball game!"

How often have they played this song at the site of the Baseball Hall of Fame in Cooperstown, N.Y. Especially on those annual occasions when the baseball world honors its outstanding players of the past who are voted into the great Hall of Fame. And how often has the vocalist used "sign language" to emphasize the words while singing—"*One, two, three strikes and you're out!*"

No question about it, baseball wouldn't be the same without the famous "Striiike!" sign. Yet, the man who invented it isn't even in the Hall of Fame. And he did much more than that. He left a record that is still unequalled and a standard of courage that is a tribute to the human spirit.

William E. Hoy was the first man with a physical handicap to succeed as a professional ball player in the major leagues. His rise to stardom began in 1887 when he played in the Northwest League and continued for 15 years of outstanding play as an outfielder for five different major league teams, including Washington, Cincinnati and Chicago.

Bill Hoy was born in Houckstown, Ohio on May 23, 1862. He lost his hearing because of a childhood illness, called "brain fever," which also deprived him of the ability to speak. He attended the Ohio School for the Deaf in Columbus, but left before he graduated in order to become a semi-professional baseball player. He was only 5 feet 5 inches tall when he began playing pro ball but he quickly showed everybody that he was a giant of an outfielder.

Hoy was one of the smartest outfielders of his time. He always seemed to know just where to throw the ball after catching it, and his accurate throwing arm frightened base-runners. This ranked him among the leaders in assists from the outfield. In 1900, while playing in 137 games for the Chicago White Sox, Hoy led the American League with 45 putout assists.

One of baseball's memorable achievements occurred on June 19, 1889 when Bill Hoy made newspaper headlines and got his name in the record book. Playing centerfield for the Washington Nationals in a game against Louisville, his rifle arm gunned down three players at home plate! And the catcher who tagged out the runners trying to score was a youngster by the name of Cornelius Mack, who later became one of baseball's legendary managers—"Connie Mack." Hoy's feat is a record that is still unequalled in major league baseball.

Bill Hoy was also an exciting base-stealer and a consistently good hitter. Playing with Cincinnati in 1888, he led the National League in stolen bases with 82 steals. Although he weighed only 150 pounds, Hoy was a powerful line-drive hitter. In a Chicago White Sox uniform, on May 1, 1901, the little outfielder from Houckstown hit a grand slam home run, the very first one hit in the newly organized American League!

During his major league career, Bill Hoy played in 1,795 games over a 15-year span. He collected 2,067 hits, for a lifetime batting average of .291. Hoy's total of 607 stolen bases, or an average of 40 steals per year, often ranked him in the top ten base-stealers.

A dazzling performer, and one with a magician's bag of tricks, Bill Hoy became a great favorite with the crowds who saw him play. The fans always enjoyed watching him perform on the field or at bat, and they had a sign language of their own for communicating with him. Whenever he made a great play (which seemed to be quite often), the crowd would cheer by standing up and waving their arms and hats wildly. They called him "The Amazing Dummy."

One little-known fact is that Bill Hoy is credited with inventing the arm signals used by home plate umpires. Unable to hear the called balls and strikes, he once asked the umpire to raise his right arm if the pitch was a "Strike." The ump agreed, and it was soon discovered that this signal not only helped Hoy, but also helped the players in the field and people in the stands who were too far away to hear. This signal became the tradition that has continued to this day. And what would America's greatest pastime be without the strike sign and the unique way every home plate umpire expresses it? For many umps, the strike sign became their personalized trademark. Without a doubt, it's something that has made the game more colorful.

When Bill Hoy died on December 15, 1961, it was just months before his 100th birthday, making him the oldest baseball player to live that long. The famous sports writer, Shirley Pov-

ich, who was also President of the Baseball Writers Association, wrote a special tribute to Hoy in his December 15th sports column of the *Washington Post* newspaper. In it, Povich reviewed Hoy's career highlights and his contributions to baseball. He also emphasized Hoy's great courage in overcoming handicaps and how he was a "model" for deaf students at Gallaudet College in Washington, D.C. They often went to see Hoy play and enjoyed his many visits to the campus, where they could "talk for hours in sign language."

In 1974, sports historian Mac Davis included a biographical sketch which immortalized the record and contributions of "Bill Hoy: The Amazing Dummy," in his book, *100 Greatest Baseball Heroes.*

Bill Hoy deserves a place in the galaxy of baseball stars. His listing in the official record book is studded with *asterisks* which show that he scored an impressive number of "firsts." He was the first deaf person to succeed in the major leagues; the first to invent the "Strike" sign for umpires; the first (and only) outfielder to throw out 3 players at home plate in one game; and the first to hit a grand slam home run in the American League. Added to these are the times he placed first, at the end of the season's play, in stealing bases and making putout assists from the outfield.

There is also that unforgettable moment, more than half a century after he played his last game with the Cincinnati Reds, when he was called upon to throw out the "first ball" in a World Series game as the oldest living alumnus of the Reds. The ball park that day was packed with people, and Joe Garagiola was describing the scene for the millions of television viewers. "Dummy Hoy . . . 99 years old!" Garagiola mused aloud on television . . . "Wonder if that's his real age or his baseball age."

As George Washington was to the people of his time, Bill Hoy was first in the hearts of his fellow deaf Americans in the realm of sports. In 1951, the American Athletic Association of the Deaf established its own "Hall of Fame" honoring outstanding deaf athletes and sports leaders. By popular and unanimous vote, the *first* deaf person to be enshrined in the "AAAD Hall of Fame" was William E. Hoy.

How many people owe their happiness to a classified advertisement in the newspaper which led them to find a job, an apartment, a used car, a pet dog? And how many others have made a nice profit from advertising their product in the "Want Ad" page? For this, they can give thanks to the man who first developed the "Want Ad" as a regular daily feature in his newspaper—William Wolcott Beadell.

Although he was totally deaf, William W. Beadell carved a brilliant career as editor and publisher of *The Observer,* a daily newspaper in Arlington, N.J., which was recognized as one of the most successful of its kind in the East. He became known as a leading advocate of truthful journalism and his editorial writings were often quoted or reprinted in other newspapers. His dedication to his life's work was so strong that, during his thirty years as owner of *The Observer,* he was absent on only two publication days.

William W. Beadell was born on December 31, 1865, in Dubuque, Iowa. Several years later, the family moved to LeMars, Iowa, where his father served as postmaster. When Beadell was eleven years old, he lost his hearing from an attack of spinal meningitis. Although he dropped out of public school, his mother taught him to become an expert lipreader.

Beadell's interest in a newspaper career began while he was a young teenager. He and a boyhood friend played in and around the printing office where his friend's father published a newspaper. Both boys began "sticking type" and learned to operate a printing press. Young Beadell soon advanced from an apprentice to city editor of the newspaper.

At the age of twenty, he decided to return to school for a while and applied for admission to the Iowa School for the Deaf. However, they found the self-taught youth too advanced for the curriculum, so he applied for admission to Gallaudet College and was accepted. He graduated in 1891, the only member of his class to reach the end of the college course and get a degree.

For a graduation gift, his father bought him a newspaper at

Yellow Creek, Illinois. The ambitious young editor wanted a more romantic name for the town—and for his newspaper. He soon influenced the citizens to change it to "Pearl City" when he found that the creek was full of clams which yielded pearls! Hence, *The Pearl City News!*

In 1895, Beadell found "the pearl of his heart" when he married Luciana Chickering, the daughter of Prof. J. W. Chickering at Gallaudet College, where the two had met. For many years thereafter, his wife served as bookkeeper or librarian for his various newspapers.

Beadell's weekly paper, *The Pearl City News,* improved in quality and interest, largely because of his shrewd management and excellent editorials. This made him decide to "go East" where he felt he would have a greater opportunity to demonstrate his ability. He sold *The Pearl City News* and moved to Middlebury, Vermont, where he became managing editor of *The Register* for the next three years.

In 1900, at the age of thirty-five, Beadell was prepared to take the most important step in his life. He purchased *The Observer*, a newspaper in Arlington, N.J., which struggled to compete with the big newspapers of nearby Jersey City, Newark, and New York. Here, he put his energy and ability to work and soon built up a rundown newspaper until it became a profit-making business.

His development of the "Want Ad" page became one of the marvels of modern journalism. Editors of magazines and newspaper publishers often asked him to write articles for their publications, explaining his method of conducting the Classified Page of *The Arlington Observer*. He also found a better method to distribute his newspaper through regular authorized newsboys who owned their own established routes or "franchises," and through local news dealers. Sales were honestly reported and the advertising agencies and bureaus knew that they could trust the circulation figures quoted by Beadell.

As busy as he was, Beadell also found time to take an active interest in the affairs of the deaf community. He contributed generously to St. Ann's Episcopal Church for the Deaf in New York as a member of the Men's Club. He waged an ongoing crusade to prove that deaf automobile drivers had a safety record as good or better than normal hearing drivers. In his own state of New Jersey, he influenced the Commissioner of the Motor Vehicle Department to repeal a ruling that was unfavorable to the deaf driver. As chief of the Automobile Bureau of the National Association of the Deaf, he collected material and data which helped the N.A.D. in fighting discrimination against deaf automobile drivers.

His untimely death, which came July 12, 1931, following an operation for appendicitis, was mourned by many people. The staff of *The Observer* paid him special tribute by printing a biographical booklet in memory of their "beloved Chief," who was one of the most prominent and respected citizens of Arlington.

Nashville, Tennessee, was once known as "the Athens of the South." Today, it is called "Music City, U.S.A." It has given instant fame to many visiting artists of recorded country music and it has been the scene of popular Hollywood films. Yet, it was one of her own native sons who first expressed the beauty of its modern skyline contour—not by means of song or screen plays but by use of drawing board and "T-square." This was the contribution of the famed deaf architect, Thomas Scott Marr.

Born on October 20, 1866 Thomas Scott Marr, Jr. came from one of the most prominent families of Nashville. His father was an established banker and three of his brothers later distinguished themselves in the fields of medicine and banking. When his hearing became severely impaired due to a childhood illness, it seemed unlikely that he could ever hope to carry on the family tradition of success.

He was first educated at the Tennessee School for the Deaf, after which he entered Gallaudet College in 1884. His roommate was a senior student, Cadwallader Washburn, who later became internationally famous as an artist. At Gallaudet, the only course related to architecture was "Mechanical Drawing" and Marr's exceptional ability in this study influenced his decision to become a draftsman. He also excelled in mathematics and the sciences, and in 1889 he graduated with honors.

His first job was for $2.50 a week as an apprentice draftsman in the office of George W. Thompson, a well-known architect of Nashville. Marr worked there for three years and then went to Boston where he took special courses of study in architecture at the Massachusetts Institute of Technology.

However, his stay at M.I.T. was cut short after only one year of study because of a sudden reversal in the family's fortunes. The United States experienced a financial panic in 1893 which affected the banking establishment as well as business, and Marr had to go back to work. When he returned to Nashville, he was welcomed back by his former employer, the senior partner of the architectural firm, Thompson and Gibel. He worked there for several years, drawing a small salary because of poor business conditions.

During these years, the young struggling architect often experienced frustration and disillusion. At one time, he almost gave up his profession, but his brother encouraged him to hold on to his dream. It turned out to be good advice because, in 1896, the economy began to improve and business was good again. By that time, too, Marr had saved $500 and was ready to use this capital to start his own architectural firm.

He also picked the right time to go into business for himself. He opened his own office in Nashville in the same year that the Tennessee State Centennial was held in his home town, in 1897, bringing both prosperity and a new optimism for the future. He soon began designing some private residential homes in Nashville and his work became widely respected for its high standards of quality and honesty.

When he was 38 years old, Marr met an ambitious young teenager, Joe Holman, who was selling magazines. Holman asked Marr for a job as office boy and said he would also like to become a draftsman. Marr gave him the job—and it turned out to be the perfect match. Marr quickly learned that Joe Holman was a "born salesman" as well as an honest and resourceful worker. After a period of apprenticeship, the young man was put to work representing the firm and soliciting contracts. The result was their merger into a partnership, Marr and Holman, in 1910.

As senior partner of the firm, Marr drew the plans, wrote specifications, and managed the architectural work. As his reputation grew, Marr became widely in demand as an architect and designed many buildings in Nashville and elsewhere in Tennessee. Among these were the *Morgan School* in Petersburg, the *Tennessee Boys Reformatory School* in Jordania, and the new *Tennessee School for the Deaf* in Knoxville. In Nashville, he designed the beautiful *Post Office Building* and three modern luxury hotels—the *Noel Hotel*, the *James Rob-*

ertson Hotel, and the *Andrew Jackson Hotel.* His designs for large apartment buildings included the *Clifton Apartments* and the *West End Apartments.*

His range of activities was so broad and his talent so versatile that he could take on almost any challenge. This was evident in his work designing two theatre structures, the *Princess Theatre* and the *Knickerbocker Theatre,* and such business establishments as the *Broadway National Bank* and the fire-proof *E.M. Bond Warehouses* in Nashville.

Early in 1936, the architectural firm of Marr and Holman was chosen by Gov. McAllister of Tennessee to draw the plans for the *State Supreme Court Building.* It was to be the last design by the grand old master.

Marr died suddenly of a stroke on March 2, 1936. A man of warm and generous nature, and with high standards of honor, he was greatly loved and admired. His reputation earned him the title, "Dean of Nashville's Architects," and many examples of his work were published in architectural textbooks that became required study in various Southern universities.

He also left no doubt about his devotion to the cause of scholarship and higher education. To future generations of deaf students at Gallaudet College, which had awarded him an Honorary Degree in 1924, he willed a large sum of money. This has now become a competitive scholarship fund, the "Thomas S. Marr Scholarship Award."

The best expression in praise of the man and his work was written by a deaf poet, Guie C. Cooke:

IN MEMORY OF THOMAS S. MARR, ARCHITECT

You built your monument up to the sky
Before you died. In sturdy stone and steel
The buildings grew, and stand, graceful and high
In clean-cut beauty, ever to reveal
The nature of a man who worked and planned
To create loveliness upon the earth;
To dream, and to design with careful hand
Foundations for the city's greater birth.
Yours was the destiny that could not swerve,
In spite of handicap, to lesser aims,
Yours were the thoughts of stately line and curve
Of structures, and your deep desire still flames.
Content with work well done, we saw you go
To build in Heaven as you built below.

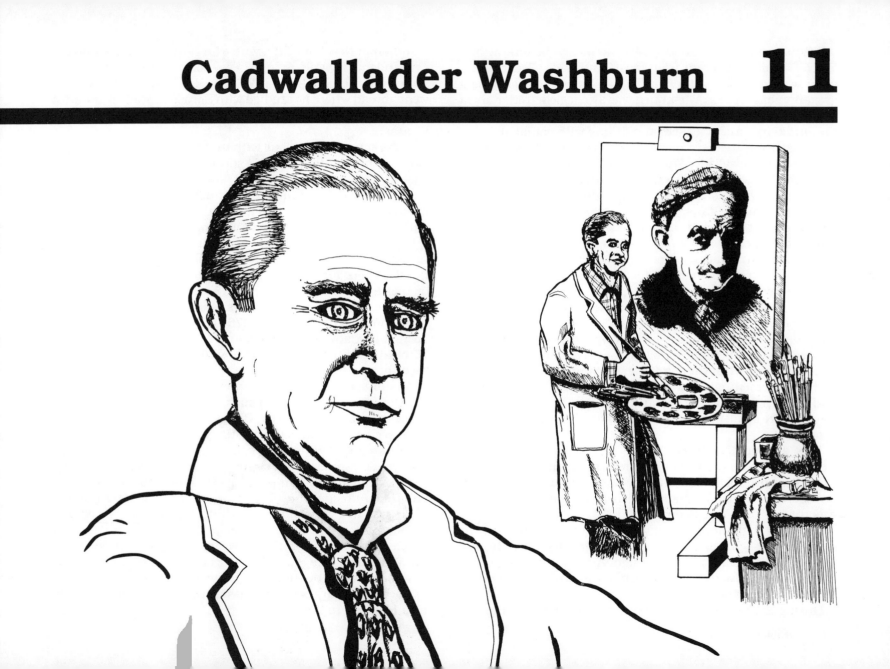

With a name like "Cadwallader," he had to be unique and special—a man different from most. And Cadwallader Washburn was just that. Although he was known primarily as a great drypoint etcher, Washburn was also a globetrotter and a daring adventurer whose experiences included interviewing revolutionary foreign leaders and dining with cannibals!

Almost from the very moment of birth, great things were expected of Cadwallader Washburn who entered the world on October 31, 1866, in Minneapolis, Minnesota. His father was a director of the Washburn-Pillsbury Flour Company and later became a United States Senator. Three of his uncles were equally distinguished, having served at various times as naval commanders, congressmen, statesmen, and ambassadors. The Washburn clan could also point with pride to other members of the family tree who had productive careers as lawyers, writers, and inventors.

It was almost as if they had placed the mantle of great expectations upon his little shoulders as soon as he learned to walk and then telling him, "Carry on, Cadwallader—Carry on!" Not only was it "a tough act to follow" but it also appeared most improbable when, at the age of five, the youngster was stricken with spinal meningitis, which left him totally deaf. However, Cadwallader was made of the stuff of champions. His handicap was just the challenge he needed to shape his own growth and destiny.

This development began at the Minnesota School for the Deaf where he showed an early interest in printing and drawing. These pre-vocational interests were pursued at Gallaudet College, from which he graduated in 1890. Among his honors was that of Class Valedictorian.

Believing that ahead of him was a career in architecture, he went to Massachusetts Institute of Technology where he was awarded a first place prize in design. After one year, however, he became convinced that his talent lay in art, so he left M.I.T. to become an artist.

During the next few years, he studied art. First, in Boston, and then in New York City, where he gained entrance into the Art Students League, despite heavy competition, and took lessons from the noted artist, William H. Chase. Eventually, he went abroad where he studied with Sorolla in Madrid and with Besnard in Paris. He also met the up-and-coming genius, Pablo Picasso.

These experiences, along with the years of training, were the basis of preparation for the special field of art he came to choose. This happened in 1900, at the time he was in Venice. There, he viewed an exhibit of etchings by the American artist, James Whistler, and he was inspired to make the change from painting with oils to dry point etching.

Dry point etching, a talent Washburn developed without the help of any instructors, is a form of engraving in which a thick needle is used for cutting into a copper plate to create a design or picture. During his lifetime, Washburn produced nearly one thousand drypoint etchings, along with many oil paintings and water colors. In 1976, Gallaudet College officially opened its Cadwallader Washburn Room. A collection of over 75 of his etchings, all donated by his wife, Margaret, can be seen there.

Washburn was an artist of international fame, and many of his works are on display in such places as the Victoria Albert Museum in London, and the Bibliothque in Paris. His etchings have been compared to the creations of such famous artists as Rembrandt and Whistler. Critics claim his portraits illumine the eyes as "windows of the soul"—such as his *Buddhist Priest*, his Mexican and Indian portraits, and his Mallorca (Spanish) subjects: *Introspection*, *The Smuggler*, and *The Matriarch*.

Art was not Washburn's only interest. He also served as a war-correspondent for the *Chicago Daily News*. In 1905, he teamed up with his brother, foreign correspondent Col. Stanley Washburn, on a journalistic "scoop" that caught the entire newspaper world by surprise. This was their eye-witness report of the peace treaty between Russia and Japan, which brought a sudden end to the war.

During the Mexican Revolution in 1910, he was given the responsibility of interviewing Francisco Madero, the Mexican president—a task no reporter had been able to accomplish because of Madero's highly mysterious and reclusive nature. Washburn knew that he would need some sort of gimmick in order to get the interview. Believing that the Mexicans might be impressed by fancy clothing, Washburn dressed himself like a modern day disco dancer. His outrageous outfit, along with his silk hat and gold-headed cane, so stunned and bewildered Madero's guards that they let Cadwallader into his office! The flamboyant deaf foreigner used a writing pad and his fluent knowledge of Spanish to pull off a very successful interview. It proved most valuable in providing information about Madero's attitudes toward the United States.

Washburn's interest in collecting rare bird eggs brought him to the Marquesas Islands, of the South Pacific, in 1925. Except for his dog, he was all alone. But not for long. During his stay, he made friends with a group of cannibals. He taught them sign language and also etched a portrait of the cannibal Chief. In return for the favors, they fed him well. But Washburn purposely stayed thin by feeding most of the food to his dog. The adventurer felt that his scrawny appearance would discourage the cannibals from trying to make *him* their next meal. His plan worked. The cannibals never tried to eat him. But nobody ever found out what happened to the dog!

Despite his daring and sometimes dangerous lifestyle, Cadwallader Washburn lived to the ripe old age of 99. He died in 1965.

The largest collection of his dry point etchings can be found at the Library of Congress in Washington, D.C., and the Metropolitan Museum of Art in New York City. The 1955 edition of *Who's Who in America* listed museums all over the world where his works are permanently exhibited, and when he died the newspaper obituaries recognized Cadwallader Washburn as "the dean of American etchers."

Imagine a San Diego Chicken who could almost pitch like Tom Seaver! That was Luther Haden Taylor, one of the most colorful baseball players to ever play in the major leagues. He was a great pitcher and a valuable player for the New York Giants when they won the National League pennant in 1904 and 1905.

Luther Taylor was born deaf on February 21, 1876 in the small town of Oaskaloosa, Kansas. After attending the Kansas School for the Deaf and graduating with honors, he began playing baseball in the semi-pro Southern League in 1898 and advanced to the Eastern League in 1900, where he won 10 games against 8 losses for the Albany, N.Y., team. The big right-hander, who stood 6'1" and weighed a sinewy 165 pounds, soon caught the eye of the New York Giants because of his blazing fast ball. The next year, he climbed to the big time with the Giants and quickly became a favorite with the great John J. McGraw, who became the Manager in 1902.

When McGraw started to build his dynasty with a Giants team that finished 25 games out of first place in 1902, he traded away every player except Christy Mathewson, Frank Bowerman, and Luther Taylor. It was McGraw who affectionately nicknamed his deaf-mute star "Dummy Taylor." John "Muggsy" McGraw and "Dummy" Taylor were natural "ham actors" who loved to excite the crowd with their antics on the field. Together with the Giants, they became one of the most colorful clubs in the majors—and one of the most feared.

The Giants, in 1904, had the best pitching staff in the majors. The team won 106 games and its "Big Three" collected 89 of that total—Joe "Iron Man" McGinnity (35 wins), Christy "Big Six" Mathewson (33), and Luther "Dummy" Taylor (21).

Dummy Taylor was a big cog in that Giants machine that won pennants in 1904 and 1905. His best year was 1904 when he won 21 games on the mound. He followed that with 16 victories in 1905 and 17 wins against only 9 losses in 1906.

At the height of his career, Taylor won the hearts of all New Yorkers. These included Broadway celebrities such as Lillian Russell, the gorgeous star of vaudeville and stage, who often went to the ball park just to see Dummy. He was very popular with the fans, who loved to see him clown around and bait the umpires by using the sign language of the deaf that nobody understood except McGraw and some of his teammates. By using sign language, he could tell the umpires that they were "blind," "crazy"—and worse. Since they could not understand him, he didn't worry about getting into trouble or being thrown out of the game.

But once the joke was on Taylor. During one game, Taylor came out of the dugout, much to the fans' delight, wearing huge rubber boots because it was raining hard. He told his teammates (in sign language, of course) that the umpire was "nuts" for not calling off the game. Everyone in the ball park was laughing at the comedy act. All of a sudden, the umpire, who had been studying Taylor carefully, walked up to him and said *in sign language:* "I know what you said! I fine you $25.00 . . . . and you're out of the game!"

It just so happened that the umpire, Hank O'Day, knew how to sign because he had a relative who was deaf. Taylor, greatly surprised and shocked, had to leave that game—the first time his act "backfired." This story, along with many other memories, was later included in McGraw's book, *My Thirty Years in Baseball.*

The only deaf pitcher to succeed in the major leagues, Dummy Taylor appeared in a total of 274 games (1901–1909). The big right-hander won 115 games and lost 106 for a .520 percentage. He pitched 160 complete games, with 767 strikeouts against 551 walks.

When Taylor "had his stuff," it was tough trying to score runs against him. A look at the records proves this much. Over a 10 year span in the majors, he allowed an average of 2.75 runs per game and hurled 21 shutouts in which he didn't allow opponents a run. Judged by modern standards, his earned run average (ERA) of 2.75 compares favorably with some of the best and highest paid pitchers in baseball today.

Taylor would also be drawing a whopping salary if he were pitching today. His colorful personality and "drawing power" would fill up the ball parks and entertain millions of television viewers.

He even had another kind of "body language" that was fascinating to watch. This was his unorthodox windup and release when in the act of pitching. It was aptly described as "a corkscrew turn" by one sportswriter, William F. Kirk, who often wrote about Taylor in *The New York American.* Once, Kirk composed a poem which vividly portrayed this colorful character. It proved to be so popular that it has often been reprinted in newspapers, magazines and baseball books:

"There's nobody else like you,
    Dummy Taylor.
You're a pitcher tried and true,
    Dummy Taylor.
When you do that corkscrew turn
And your speed begins to burn,

You create profound concern,
    Dummy Taylor.
Yesterday you made 'em stare,
    Dummy Taylor,
When your foemen fanned the air,
    Dummy Taylor.
Air was what they mostly struck—
Now and then they raked the muck—
And 'twas not a case of luck,
    Dummy Taylor.
As a talker, you'll never shine,
    Dummy Taylor,
But full many a friend of mine,
    Dummy Taylor,
Could secure the world's regard
If he didn't talk so hard
And performed like you, old pard,
    Dummy Taylor."

When his fastball began to fade and he left the Giants in 1909, the team showed its appreciation by giving him a solid gold medal with 20 diamonds. Several years later, the major leagues honored him with a lifetime silver pass, giving him free admission to all baseball games.

Taylor returned to the minor leagues where he still was able to compete successfully at that level. For the next 6 years, he pitched for Buffalo (Eastern League), Montreal (International League), and Brantford (Canadian League). Finally, his arm gave out and his professional career came to an end in 1914.

It was the beginning of a new career, however, not as a player but as a coach. For more than 20 years afterwards, Taylor served as Athletic Coach at both the Kansas School for the Deaf and the Iowa School for the Deaf where his teams ran up outstanding records in both baseball and football. He not only spoke their language but he was also a born leader, with the charisma to inspire teenage athletes and draw out their potential skills as individuals and as a team. At his alma mater, the Kansas School, he so fired up his teams that they would often spring upsets—beating college level opponents such as Ottawa University, William Jewel College, Rockhurst College, and Baker University.

When he began to feel the aches and pains of coaching, Taylor closed out another chapter of his life—only to begin a new one. He went to the Illinois School for the Deaf in Jacksonville, where he spent the next 18 years as a dormitory counselor and consultant to athletic programs. Upon his retirement at the age of 65, he was contacted again by his old team, the N.Y. Giants, and he became a baseball scout in their organization. In 1952, the American Athletic Association of the Deaf honored Taylor by making him the second deaf person elected to the "AAAD Hall of Fame."

Luther Haden Taylor passed away on August 22, 1958. It was a warm summer afternoon, about the time when baseball games are over and the scoreboard shows the final score. It marked the end to the colorful career of one of "the boys of summer." But to all those who knew him, and to the world of baseball, he will always be affectionately remembered as the one and only "Dummy Taylor."

Although much attention has been given to minorities since the 1960s, one group that continues to be ignored and cut off from the mainstream is the American Indian. Much like the deaf, American Indians have had to endure society's misconceptions about them for centuries. The deaf quietly, and sometimes not so quietly, tolerated the "deaf and dumb" label, and all the connotations that went with it, ever since it was first used by Aristotle and the ancient Greeks. The American Indian, even in this enlightened and modern age, is still branded "savage" by people who prefer to be conned by myth.

Perhaps it was from this shared sense of being misunderstood by society that George Hyde, a deaf man, established an instant friendship with the first Indians he met in his teens, and later became an Indian historian dedicated to telling the Indian's side of history. His extensive and innovative research of various American Plains Indian tribes that populated the West, such as the Sioux and Cheyenne, provide the kind of chronicles that forever will be valued. Anyone looking for an objective account of American Plains Indian culture and history should consult George Hyde's many books.

George Hyde was born in Omaha, Nebraska on June 10, 1882. As a boy living in the wide-open spaces of the frontier, he was fascinated by tales about legendary figures that have shaped and flavored American history, names such as Sitting Bull, Buffalo Bill, Geronimo, Crazy Horse, and General Custer. After meeting a few Indians who were attending the 1898 "Trans-Mississippi Exposition" in Omaha, Hyde was invited to their camps and quickly became fascinated by their rich culture. The visit marked the beginning of a long and trustworthy relationship between Hyde and his Indian neighbors.

While growing up in Omaha, George Hyde literally played "hide and seek" with the public school system. Most of the time, he could be found in libraries, reading about Indians and the Wild West. His introversion was partly due to a mysterious physical disorder which impaired his hearing and eyesight. By the time he was twenty-one, his hearing was totally gone and his eyesight very poor. Realizing the limitations that his handicaps put on him, Hyde decided to become a writer and concentrate on the subject that had always been the most interesting to him—Indian culture.

His first professional assignment was as an assistant to George Bird Grinnell, a well-known ethnologist. Grinnell was interested in investigating the Cheyenne tribe and he employed Hyde because of Hyde's knowledge about them. Their combined effort resulted in the book, *The Fighting Cheyennes* (1915). The fact that the two men went directly to the Cheyennes for information, rather than depend entirely on researching "official documents" found in libraries and archives, was the beginning of a new approach toward Indian research. No longer would "the Indian story" be told by using second and third-hand reports based on hearsay, superstition, and prejudice. Hyde's insistence on the importance of using Indian eyewitnesses if possible, or at least getting their version of things, guaranteed a more objective and balanced reflection on the past. The Indian's side of a story would have to be considered, Hyde argued, if history were to be told accurately. This responsible and humane attitude gained the deaf writer much respect from other professionals in the field. It also strengthened his relationship with the Indians.

Hyde's next study resulted in the book *Corn Among the Indians of the Upper Missouri* (1917), which described Indian agricultural techniques and mythology. In 1920, because of increasing blindness, his half-sister, Mabel Reed, began caring for him and shared her income as a school teacher. Although his handicaps made communication more difficult, Hyde continued to research and write. He collected most of his information through correspondence with Indian friends and acquaintances. When direct contact was necessary, he used pen, pad and magnifying glass to receive communication. The many friends Hyde made since that Trans-Mississippi Exposition back in 1898 helped him get information when travel was impossible.

Hyde's major contribution as a historian was his trilogy on the Sioux, considered by many to be the most thorough study ever done on a Plains Indian tribe. The trilogy—*Red Cloud's Folk* (1937); *A Sioux Chronicle* (1956); and *Spotted Tail's Folk* (1961)—is grand in scope, tracing the history of the Sioux from 1660 through the tragedy at Wounded Knee, South Dakota, where the bravest of the braves died in the snow on December 29, 1890.

Both *Red Cloud's Folk* and *Spotted Tail's Folk* are included in Anna Lee Stensland's comprehensive bibliography, *Literature by and about the American Indian*. In her book, Stensland praises Hyde and his role in Indian scholarship as a kind of myth-breaker. Noting that, over the years, many Indian leaders such as Sitting Bull, Spotted Tail, and Crazy Horse typically have been "maligned by biographers of warlike chiefs," Stensland admiringly mentions Hyde's uncommon attempt in *Spotted Tail's Folk* to present the Sioux Chief as a great and noble individual intent on "saving his people without fighting the white man."

Stensland is not alone in her acclaim. Vine Deloria, distinguished author and professor of Indian studies (and a Sioux himself), called *Spotted Tail's Folk* an "outstanding book" in his introduction to *Indians of the Americas* by Edwin Embree.

Some of George Hyde's other works include *Indians of the High Plains* (1959); and *Indians of the Woodlands: From Prehistoric Times to 1725*, published three years later. His last book, *Life of George Bent, Written from His Letters*, was based on correspondence with one of his closest Indian friends. The date of publication was 1968, the same year George Hyde died of cancer at the age of eighty-five.

Although his life was a difficult one, Hyde always maintained a cheerful disposition, complemented by wit and charm. He spent his entire life in Omaha and made many friends, both Indian and white. Both groups remember him as a man on a quest for truth. Despite what some might call his "strong allegiance" to the Indians, Hyde refrained from over-exuberantly romanticizing them in his writing, for to do so would have made his work as flawed as the "official documents" he used only as supplements, never as gospel. His many books are objective and honest accounts of a misunderstood race forced into oppression. His work has become precious over the years, helping historians, anthropologists, film-makers, students, and others better understand the beauty and tragedy of the American Plains Indian.

Fate plays strange tricks on people in the game of life. Take the case of LeRoy Colombo. A champion long-distance swimmer, with the handsome face and the body of an Adonis, he might have become a Hollywood star in movies portraying the role of "Tarzan." Unfortunately, it never happened because he was totally deaf. Yet, this very same handicap made LeRoy Colombo become all the more determined to excel as a swimmer and be of service to people in need. So well did he succeed that not only was he the first deaf person to become a life guard but he also went on to become the world's greatest life saver!

LeRoy Colombo was born on December 23, 1905, in Galveston, Texas, the island city situated on the Gulf of Mexico. At the age of seven he became totally deaf from an attack of spinal meningitis, which also caused paralysis in his legs. His recovery from this disease was long and painful, during which his brothers, Nick and Cinto, helped him with the only physical therapy he ever received. Everyday, they dragged him up and down the alley behind their house, trying to make him walk again. When he regained some strength in his legs, Nick and Cinto began taking him to the beach. He quickly learned to swim and felt more at home in water than on land. Gradually, the strength returned to his legs and he was able to walk again.

At the age of eight, LeRoy attended a public school in Galveston. However, he was unable to keep up with all the normal hearing children there, so he dropped out several months later. When he was twelve, he went to the Texas School for the Deaf in Austin where he learned to read lips and communicate in sign language. He also perfected his swimming in the school's indoor pool where he swam daily for hours. It helped build up his body and his stamina so that he became as strong as a bull.

By the time he was sixteen, Colombo had become an expert swimmer. The people who went to the beach at Galveston started noticing him because he could swim for hours and hours. One day, his brother, Cinto, asked the Surf Club if LeRoy could become a member. The selective Club said that he must first pass a test in which he would have to swim for three hours without stopping or floating on his back. Colombo passed the test with ease and became the first deaf person to join the exclusive Surf Club. In the same year, he also became a full-fledged Life Guard for the City of Galveston.

One year later, Colombo took on another challenge. This was more like a showdown. He had to compete against Herbert Brenan, the national endurance champion of the Amateur Athletic Union. Brenan was known as the man who could swim longer than anyone else without stopping. LeRoy Colombo beat him. The next year, the two men had a re-match in a ten mile race. Again, LeRoy won, defeating Brenan by a full mile and setting a new record for Galveston by completing the race in six hours and fifty-five minutes.

Another time, LeRoy and his brother, Cinto, took first and second place honors in a 15-mile marathon race. The Colombo brothers were the only two men to finish the marathon, during which all the contestants had to struggle against strong ocean currents and changing tides. LeRoy was timed at 11 hours and 30 minutes, beating his brother by 3½ hours.

When he was twenty-three, LeRoy swam 30 miles in 16 hours and 24 minutes. Between the years of 1929 and 1939, he won all the distance races held in the Gulf of Mexico.

Being only human, there were times when LeRoy lost a race. In one event, held at St. Louis in 1926, he competed in a 10 mile race in the Mississippi River. He dislocated a shoulder after the eighth mile and swam the last two miles with one arm. He didn't win that one, but he finished. Another young swimmer, Johnny Weismuller, who was an Olympic champion and later became famous in the movies as *Tarzan*, was also in that race—and failed to finish.

During all these years, Colombo was also doing a great service to mankind—saving people's lives. Beginning with the summer when he was only twelve years old and saved the life of a drowning boy, Colombo regularly made headlines in the Galveston newspapers and his name was on the lips of all

from drowning. They even said he had "twice the nine lives of a cat" because Colombo almost drowned 16 times himself. This happened whenever the drowning person got a panic armlock around Colombo's neck—but he always managed to work himself free and save the frightened person.

As the years passed, Colombo became known as the "Hero of Galveston." During his forty years as a life guard, he saved the lives of 907 people—an achievement that is now listed in the *Guiness Book of World Records!*

He seldom got any money for his brave deeds but he was known and loved by thousands of people. They found it easy to communicate with the deaf life guard who talked with his whole body as well as with voice. A skilled pantomimist, with a salty sense of humor, Colombo enjoyed kidding with those people who sought his company at beautiful Galveston Beach. They came from all parts of America—farmers, school teachers, gamblers, millionaires, and Broadway celebrities such as Alice Faye, Phil Harris and Ben Bernie.

He retired at the age of 65 but he continued to hang around with old friends and assorted characters on Galveston Beach. The lure of the sea was irresistible, and he found swimming much easier than walking. In fact, as Jane Kenamore, the Archivist at the Rosenberg Library of Galveston attests, "he was still swimming a mile a day in the Gulf (summer and winter!) up until a few weeks before he died."

At the time of his death, July 12, 1974, Senator A. R. Schwartz of Galveston introduced a resolution honoring him in the Texas legislature and its members stood for a moment of silence. In many parts of the state, the flag of Texas was lowered at half mast in his memory. The people of Galveston showed their appreciation by erecting a special landmark with a plaque on the beach that he used to patrol. It commemorates LeRoy Colombo's dedication to duty and his peerless record of saving the lives of 907 people.

reporters. They told of how, in March, 1928, the tugboat *Propeller* exploded in flames and how Colombo swam beneath burning oil to rescue two crewmen. They told of how he once rescued a fireman trapped on top of a burning building and how he later received a city commendation for his courage. And, still another time, they told about that winter day when he dived into the icy waters of Galveston Bay to save two men

"Rain, rain, go away,
Little Hillis wants to play—
Come again some other day!"

If his mother had sung this rhyme for little Hillis Arnold on that particular day in the Spring of 1916, it surely must have been in vain. Her words not only "fell on deaf ears," but little Hillis was already outside the family farm house in North Dakota, standing in mud up to his ankles! The sight of one of their cows, sunk even deeper in the mud, had caught his attention. Almost as quickly as the idea came to mind, he scooped up some mud in his hands and began shaping little mud figures.

When his mother came outside, she was more than a bit surprised at what she saw. She thought the mud figures were most interesting, and it gave her an idea. She decided to buy her ten year old son some modeling clay so that he could keep busy with a new hobby. Little did she dream that her little deaf boy would someday become one of the finest sculptors in America!

N. Hillis Arnold was born in 1906. A victim of spinal meningitis, he became totally deaf at the age of six months. His parents wanted him to learn to speak and lipread but were unable to find a school in North Dakota which could provide an oral education. When Hillis was twelve, the family moved to Minneapolis and enrolled him in the Minneapolis Day School for the Deaf. He progressed so well that he was later mainstreamed into Minneapolis Central High School, from which he graduated with honors. After high school, he entered the University of Minnesota, and in 1933, he was graduated *cum laude.*

Having decided on his chosen field of interest, Arnold pursued his studies in sculpture at the Minneapolis School of Art and, later, at the Cranbrook Academy of Art in Bloomfield Hills, Michigan. At Cranbrook, he had the good fortune to study with Carl Milles, the famed Swedish sculptor, who was quick to judge his talent. Milles offered Arnold the opportunity to assist him in creating the beautiful fountain display at Union Station Park, in St. Louis. It was named *The Wedding of the Rivers* to symbolize the union of the Missouri and the Mississippi.

In 1938, Arnold accepted a position as instructor of sculpture at Monticello College, a private junior college for women in Alton, Illinois. To communicate more clearly with his students, he attended night classes for adults at the Central Institute for the Deaf in nearby St. Louis, taking advanced lessons in speech and lipreading. Thereafter, he had few problems in communicating with students at Monticello. If anything became too complex or abstract, he let his hands express it for him! His position at Monticello also gave him the opportunity to do what he most desired in life—to teach and work as a free lance artist.

Over the past fifty years, Hillis Arnold has emerged as one of the most productive sculptors in the Midwest. He is also one of the most versatile in America, working in almost every known media—marble, stone, wood, clay and various metals. His creations, too, are as widely different in form and expression.

Several of his most popular works are in the St. Louis area. One is the *World War II Memorial* in Aloe Plaza. Standing 32 feet high, this imposing limestone shaft depicts Army soldiers on one side and Navy soldiers on the other side—leaving home, in combat, and emerging from death. Another is the great *American Eagle*, made of walnut, whose five foot wing span expresses the theme of "Manifest Destiny" in the Museum of Westward Expansion underneath the St. Louis Arch. Two other statues, six feet tall, are in a junior high school located in nearby LaDue. These feature Mark Twain's favorite characters, *Tom Sawyer and Huckleberry Finn,* in a comic scene from the novel.

Arnold's work is in great demand by the church and clergy. Cardinal Joseph Ritter of St. Louis purchased two of his masterpieces, which were placed in the Cardinal's private residence in LaDue. One of these, an abstract interpretation of *The Lord Is My Shepherd,* is made of Georgia marble and

make them lighter in weight, easier to move around, and less costly to produce. One of these plastic aluminum marvels is the 9 foot statue of *Christ* for the Gustavus Adolphus Church in St. Paul, Minnesota. Another medium he has used successfully is polyester resin with which he designed an *angel,* chosen by the U.S. Information Agency for its "Plastics, USA" cultural exchange exhibit that went on tour throughout Russia and Europe. A five foot model of this *angel* is now located at the Sisters of Mercy Chapel in Frontenac, Missouri.

Hillis Arnold is today a Professor Emeritus of Sculpture, having retired in 1974 from Monticello College (now Lewis and Clark Community College). With his wife and two daughters, he lives in Kirkwood, Missouri, where he continues to do free lance work and contribute to community interests in art. Among his many honors, he holds the title of Live Fellow of the International Institute of Arts and Letters, which recognizes him as one of the finest sculptors in America.

In 1983, at 77 years of age, he was still as creative as ever and very much in the public eye. This was evident in his one man show, held at the Towata Gallery in Alton, Illinois, April 10–May 8, 1983. Entitled, "Hillis Arnold Sculpture Exhibit," it featured various sculptures in terra cotta, metals, wood and stone as well as photographs and small models of many of his larger works now located in Kansas, Illinois, Minnesota, and Wisconsin. One of these new creations is a small marble of a mother and child, a model for the full-scale sculpture *The Learners* at the Central Institute for the Deaf. As reviewed by art critic Patricia Degener in the *St. Louis Post-Dispatch* (May 1, 1983) the statue expresses Arnold's childhood, his spirit and success as an artist despite his deafness. It also depicts his mother's determination that he should learn to speak. "Patiently she taught him and that part of the teaching, the feeling of vibrations in the chest made by the vocal cords, is the subject of the sculpture."

It also conveys his special gift of perception. "Because I am deaf," Arnold said, "I am a better observer."

stands 7 feet high in the garden. The other is the two-and-a-half foot statue of Abraham and Issac, carved and polychromed in mahogany wood, placed in the Cardinal's chapel. A beautiful work of religious art, *Abraham and Issac* was previously displayed at the national exhibit of the Religious Art Center of America, in Latrobe, Pennsylvania, and later at the International Biennale of Contemporary Christian Art in Salzburg, Austria (1948).

Two other outstanding works by Arnold are in Normandy, a suburb of St. Louis. His 16-foot limestone statue of St. Mary and St. Anne, *Mother and Child Mary,* above the entrance of St. Anne's Catholic Church, was later featured in *Time* and *Life* magazines. His 8 ft. double doors in bronze, a resplendent work of craftsmanship for the Normandy Presbyterian Church, also won second place at the annual convention of the Church Architectural Guild of America.

Arnold has also made bold use of experimentation. He has pioneered the use of plastic aluminum in his sculptures to

'20s '30s

'40s '50s

'60s '70s

'80s

The overhead lights dim and a hushed silence descends upon the ballroom. The sound of music fills the air and the spotlight focuses on "The Wonder Dancers." The man is tall, dark and handsome, and the woman is a golden beauty whose radiance outshines the gilded sequins of her gown. As they swing and sway to the rhythm of the rhumba, they are so picture perfect that it is almost like looking at a scene in a movie featuring Fred Astaire and Ginger Rogers.

A quick look at the printed programme, however, reminds the audience that they are being entertained by one of the most unusual dance teams ever seen—Frances Woods and Billy Bray. They are unique because Frances Woods cannot hear a single note of music; she is totally deaf. But there is rhythm in her soul and her whole body is alive with music. She can feel the cadence through vibrations of the dance floor, and even when dancing on a floor of marble, she can sense the flow and beat of rhythm through her fingertips.

The life story of Frances Woods could easily become the inspiration for a Hollywood movie about overcoming handicaps.

When Esther Thomas was born on March 21, 1907, in Girard, Ohio, her doctor didn't expect her to live. A premature baby, she weighed only 1½ pounds at birth. It was also discovered that she was born without ear drums.

However, little Esther Thomas survived and she grew up to be strong and athletic. At the Ohio School for the Deaf, in Columbus, she played center on the girl's basketball team for five winning seasons. During the summer's vacation from school in 1924, she met Anthony Caligiure, a handsome young dancer who looked like Rudolph Valentino. They literally fell in love on the dance floor where they rehearsed—in her father's garage!

As their romance blossomed, they went to many dances during the next two summers and won several awards for their performances. When Tony asked for her hand in marriage, her mother consented but her father refused. He felt that his daughter should marry someone who was also deaf. However, after she graduated from the Ohio School, her father changed

his mind and the young lovers were married on September 5, 1926.

As husband and wife, Tony and Esther worked hard to develop a variety of dance acts and routines in preparation for their professional career. With great patience and skill, Tony taught Esther by playing the piano and getting her to feel the 4/4 time or 3/4 time of the music. Then he would teach her the dance steps to follow the particular rhythm.

"Body language" was not the only way they communicated with each other. She taught him fingerspelling and sign language, and he helped greatly to improve her ability to speak and lipread. He also became her interpreter, and the result was that they were able to interact freely and communicate with both the deaf and hearing.

They were first known as "The Dancing DeSondos" when

they began to dance professionally. Later, in 1928, C. B. Maddock of New York who was the producer of many big shows on Broadway gave them the stage names of "Frances Woods and Billy Bray." Not long afterwards, they caught the eye of Robert L. Ripley, the famous cartoonist of "Ripley's Believe It Or Not," who featured them in his newspaper column and called them "The Wonder Dancers."

Success didn't come easily during their early years in show business. First came "the Stock Market Crash" in 1929, and then "the Great Depression" began. Millions of people were unemployed, money was very scarce, and the entertainment business suffered. Woods and Bray, "The Wonder Dancers," practically lived out of a single suitcase and were often down to their last dollar.

Like born troupers, however, they kept their act together and "went on with the show." Their big break came in the early 1930's when R.K.O Productions booked "The Wonder Dancers" to perform in vaudeville acts. One of these was "The Adagio," an exciting dance number which includes acrobatic feats of the kind seen in circuses. Another was the "French Apache," a combination of dance and mime.

Although they became known as one of the greatest combos performing the "Adagio" and the "Apache," Woods and Bray developed a versatile program that included all the popular dances of the times—the Fox Trot, the Waltz, the Tango, the Rhumba, and the Samba. For each of these dances, Frances Woods designed and made all her own clothes and costumes. Indeed, it was not unusual for her to make a dress with 26,000 sequins, sewed on one at a time.

Through the 1930's, the Forties and the Fifties, Woods and Bray appeared in most of the major night clubs and hotels. They were accompanied by all the great "big bands"—Wayne King, Ted Weems, Cab Calloway, Eddie Duchin, Horace Heidt, Paul Whiteman, and many others. They performed at the Edgewater Hotel in Chicago when Lawrence Welk had his first major engagement. And Welk still credits Billy Bray with helping him to become the fine dancer he is.

"The Wonder Dancers" have performed in Europe, often appearing at the famed "Palladium" in London. Extended engagements at the Shoreham Hotel in Washington made them favorites with the government social set, and their admirers include many great and prominent people.

Many honors have come to Woods and Bray, but their greatest satisfaction is in reaching out to the young and old who look up to them for inspiration and cheer. This has been their mission during their "retirement years." Nothing delights them more than giving dance lessons to school children in their hometown of Youngstown, Ohio. They take the same pleasure in traveling all over the country to uplift senior citizens, people in nursing homes, and handicapped persons. For this, they were honored at the Governor's Awards Banquet, February 9, 1978, which recognized Ohio natives and residents whose careers have benefitted mankind and brought honor to the state. Sharing honors with Woods and Bray that evening were actor Hugh O'Brian; Susan Perkins, 1978 "Miss America"; Jim Marshall, "All-Pro" defensive end of the Minnesota Vikings; and George M. Steinbrenner, Chairman of the American Shipbuilding Co., and owner of the New York Yankees.

To look at them today, no one would believe that Frances Woods and Billy Bray have been dancing together for over 55 years, or ever since they were married in 1926. People would also find it hard to believe that Frances Woods has a heart problem which makes it necessary for her to wear a mechanical heart device, known as a "pacemaker." She first had one implanted in 1968, at the age of 61, and she is now dancing to the rhythm of the fourth pacemaker for her heart—and still going strong!

Today, the wax look-alikes of Woods and Bray are in the Ripley Museum. "The Wonder Dancers" they were—and still are! The tango, the samba, the rhumba—just name the dance and they can do the call—encore!

He was born in Wisconsin, not far from the home of the Green Bay Packers. His idols were Curly Lambeau and Johnny Blood, two of the greatest players on the Green Bay team that was making ready to dominate the newly-established National Football League with successive championships in 1929–30–31. As a football star on his own high school team in Racine, he already had dreams of someday making it with the Packers. Suddenly, in his senior year, disaster struck. At the very time he was in training for the coming football season. An attack of spinal meningitis not only caused total deafness but also seriously impaired his balance.

As further irony, his own father, who was a doctor, was helpless to do anything more than be thankful that his son didn't die from the dreaded disease. He could only hope and pray that the youth would recover and someday amount to something in life. Not in football, of course, but maybe in some other worthwhile profession.

The way things turned out for Boyce Williams, it was just what the doctor ordered. Boyce returned to high school and graduated one year later. Not knowing where to go or what to do, he began to feel lonely and depressed. His father suggested that he go to the Wisconsin School for the Deaf for advice and rehabilitation. Boyce, however, "turned a deaf ear" to his father's words, feeling it beneath his dignity to go to "an asylum for the mentally ill" (as he regarded the School in those days). Dr. Williams consulted a field worker who described the School—and added that it had a fine *sports program*. That was the clincher which hooked young Williams!

Once again, it proved to be ironic at how things turned out for young Williams. He became all the things he least expected to be.

Starting with the Wisconsin School for the Deaf, he learned sign language; he also developed an awareness of the communication problems that many deaf people experience, in school and in life. Years later, Williams became Director of the Office of Communicative Disorders, in the U.S. Department of Health, Education and Welfare. As the director of vocational training at the Indiana School for the Deaf, he learned to value the role played by the field worker or specialist who tries to help deaf persons in need of guidance and counseling, vocational training and placement, social adjustment, and mental health. Eventually, all these services became a major share of his responsibilities when he rose to the position of Consultant to the Deaf in the Rehabilitation Services Administration, DHEW.

Boyce R. Williams was born in Racine, Wisconsin, on August 29, 1910. Totally deafened at the age of seventeen, he returned to Racine High School and graduated in 1928. After attending the Wisconsin School for the Deaf, he applied for admission to Gallaudet College and was accepted in the fall of 1929.

At Gallaudet, Williams quickly demonstrated that he was a man in a hurry. He not only "skipped" two years by dint of superior achievement in the classroom but he also helped the football team run over opponents on the gridiron. Williams stood out in the backfield as a smart and gutsy blocking back who helped his teammates find holes in the opposing line. It was more than mere coincidence, moreover, that Gallaudet's "Blue Bisons" thundered through two winning seasons at the same time the Green Bay Packers were dominating the NFL in 1929–30–31. In 1930, particularly, Gallaudet's record of 6-1-1 was one of the best in its long history of football.

Williams graduated from college in 1932 and found employment the next year as a teacher at the Wisconsin School for the Deaf. Although this was the period of "the Great Depression" and a time when most teachers were happy to "stay put," Williams was still on an accelerated time table. Two years later, he visited the Indiana School for the Deaf in search of job advancement. He was interviewed by the principal, Hilda Tillinghast, a woman with normal hearing who was the fourth generation of a family that had pioneered in the founding and growth of schools for the deaf in the United States and Canada. He not only secured a teaching position but he also got a lock on the principal. They were married one year later.

As Shakespeare writes, in *Julius Caesar:*

> "There is a tide in the affairs of men
> Which, taken at the flood, leads on to fortune. . ."

Whether or not the ex-football player found the time to study Shakespeare, he nevertheless knew what to do when opportunity knocks. At the age of 27, Boyce Williams became director of vocational training at the Indiana School for the Deaf, a position he held until 1945. During summer vacations, he took courses at Marquette University and then studied at Columbia University in New York, receiving a master's degree in education in 1940.

With a background in vocational training and education of the deaf, Williams was ready to make his next move. It was 1945, and World War II had finally come to an end. Williams was quick to perceive that vocational rehabilitation services, although in existence for 25 years, had finally made a breakthrough by training thousands of disabled persons for war production, including deaf people. In other words, employers finally learned that disabled people could become excellent workers, with proper training and placement.

Although many deaf people had contributed dramatically to the war effort, Williams foresaw what would happen as returning servicemen came back home to claim their old jobs. Deaf people would be the first to be laid off. Worse still, they would have an even tougher time in finding employment because of their communication problems and the need of training for different kinds of work. He responded to this need by "fighting fire with fire."

No deaf person had previously held office within the national Rehabilitation Services Administration in Washington, D.C. In 1945, Boyce Williams applied for such a position but was rejected because of his deafness. He wrote letters of appeal to the President's office but was told to try the Civil Service Commission. According to their policy at the time, the Civil Service would not even consider a hard of hearing person for the job Williams wanted.

Like a smart coordinator of offensive plays in football, Williams decided on a new game plan. He took a job with the Division of Vocational Rehabilitation back home in Indianapolis for several months. This established his qualification, from the Civil Service point of view. In the fall of 1945, he was accepted on the Federal level for the position of Consultant for the Deaf, the Hard of Hearing and the Speech Impaired.

The first ten years of service with the Federal vocational office and the State vocational agencies were mostly learning experiences for Williams. These programs were on a much smaller scale at that time and most of his work was committed to activities other than national program development. Even then, however, Williams pioneered the movements which promoted deaf rehabilitations. He worked hard to convince the State agencies that deaf clients must be served by counselors able to communicate in sign language and that training services be especially adapted to deaf persons. He also established cooperative agreements with all of the program oriented organizations in the broad field of communicative disorders, including the National Association of the Deaf.

Williams played a key role in the phenomenal growth and success of the NAD, beginning with 1964. If Fred Schrieber was the Executive Director and the man who ran the show, Boyce Williams was the NAD's "Broadway angel" who helped provide the vital grants-in-aid for its developing programs. It was largely Williams' influence that the Federal rehabilitation office sponsored the Workshop on Interpreting for the Deaf, held at Ball State Teachers College in Muncie, Indiana, 1964, with the purpose of providing better interpreting and translating services for the deaf. The NAD was given the responsibility to direct this ongoing project which eventually evolved into a national organization, the Registry of Interpreters for the Deaf. Other major undertakings by the NAD, which were the result of Federal grants from Williams' office, included the International Research Conference on the Vocational Rehabilitation of Deaf Persons, held in Washington, D.C., in 1968; the National Census of the Deaf Population completed in 1971; the World Congress of the Deaf, hosted by the NAD at Washington in 1975; and the projects to promote and implement sign language training through the NAD's Communicative Skills Program, which is now highly successful on a nation-wide scale. The result of all this "seed money" proved mutually advantageous. NAD involvement in such large scale research and development projects also helped infuse new energy and spirit in rehabilitation work.

Rome wasn't built in one day, and all this didn't happen overnight. Neither did Boyce Williams do it alone. He was aided no little by the enactment of new federal laws and amendments which greatly expanded vocational rehabilitation services and allowed for important specialization among most federal rehabilitation workers. In this he was also encouraged by the late Dr. Mary E. Switzer, who became Commissioner of RSA during the 1960's. A staunch supporter of the deaf and hard of hearing, Dr. Switzer provided the kind of enlightened and dynamic leadership which often gave high priority to their needs.

Mary Switzer had a long and distinguished career of federal service, starting as a junior economist in the Treasury Department. She had the highest regard for her deaf colleague who had also earned national recognition for his work in the federal service. Together, they made a winning combination as they went on to identify and implement effective program development. These programs often provided wholesome spin-off benefits to the deaf community, as a whole. A notable example is the National Theatre of the Deaf, first proposed as "an idea whose time has come," in 1963.

Switzer and Williams were quick to see the potential of the NTD proposal which was later submitted by David Hays, the noted Broadway scenic designer, and which had the support of deaf cultural leadership and such hearing professionals as

Dr. Edna Levine, the highly regarded psychologist of the deaf. Not only would a touring company of deaf professionals break ground vocationally for talented deaf persons, it would also bring living theatre to a deprived deaf community.

The NTD proposal was approved by the Vocational Rehabilitation Administration in 1966 and provided with a funding grant of $336,000 for the first five years of operation. The NTD proposal also included provision for an annual Summer School Program which would offer young deaf adults the opportunity to receive comprehensive training in acting and play production, as well as encourage further study and activity in movements related to school and community theatre of the deaf.

Under the guiding genius of David Hays, the National Theatre of the Deaf has since become a most successful model of social and vocational rehabilitation. It has awakened the sense of pride in deaf people, and it has entertained millions of others—in the theatre and on television. In their hands, the sign language of the so-called "deaf and dumb" is transformed (like "The Ugly Duckling") into "a many-splendored thing"—a form of visual expression which paints pictures in the air and suits the action to the word (as Hamlet advised the actors in Shakespeare's play). Similarly, whenever they "do their own thing," NTD has presented deafness in positive ways to people unfamiliar with it. They have dramatized "the deaf experience" with such honest realism as to win friends and influence people all over the world.

The National Theatre of the Deaf is only one example of the many successful programs supported by the RSA and which have affirmed Williams' belief that deaf people can be anything they want to be, if they have full access to their special mode of communication and expression. For the same reason, Williams has steadily maintained that the counselor has the most important role in the rehabilitation office. The counselor must be able to communicate effectively whenever a deaf person applies for help—whether for job training or advancement, continuing or higher education, speech therapy or sign language training, or just to get a new hearing aid so as to function better on the job and in society. The scope and range of rehabilitation services are continually broadening in the attempt to meet these special needs. The number of deaf persons receiving VR help each year has increased from a range of 500–800 in the 1940's to 5,500–7,500 in the late 1960's. By 1980, there were 20,000–25,000 deaf rehabilitations annually.

These figures do not tell the whole story of how Boyce Williams has contributed to the rehabilitation movement throughout the years. They do not account for the many times he has assembled and directed Task Forces composed of professional and voluntary consultants to develop recommendations on the vocational rehabilitation of persons with communication problems, nor the hundreds of follow up workshops which he coordinated at the State, regional, and national level. Neither do these figures reveal the "success stories" of many deaf and hearing persons who have benefitted from professional training programs in colleges and rehabilitation facilities.

An outstanding example is the program conducted by the National Center on Deafness at California State University, Northridge. In 1960, CSUN received a planning grant from Rehabilitation Services Administration to design a graduate level "National Leadership Training Program in the Area of the Deaf," which was implemented two years later. Professionals in the field of deafness (teachers, rehabilitation counselors, school counselors) receive the training necessary to develop leadership skills and move into administrative positions. This comprehensive course of study for a small group of select individuals, deaf and hearing, includes a variety of practical field experiences and leads to a Master's degree in Educational Administration Supervision and Higher Education. Under the dynamic leadership of its director, Dr. Ray L. Jones, the National Leadership Training Program has seen its graduates become program coordinators, supervisors, school principals and superintendents throughout the nation and abroad. Above all,

it exemplifies Williams' ongoing efforts to provide upward mobility for deaf persons seeking to raise their level of career aspirations.

Although Boyce Williams never did get to play for the Green Bay Packers or win a "Super Bowl" ring, he has since accumulated enough honors and awards to decorate a whole locker room. In 1958, he received an Honorary Doctor of Laws degree from Gallaudet College and in 1972 he was awarded an Honorary Doctor of Humane Letters degree by Carthage College in his home state of Wisconsin. His list of Distinguished Service Awards is both laudable and lengthy. Among these are the Award of Merit from the International Congress on Education of the Deaf, the Bell Greve Memorial Award from the National Rehabilitation Association, the award for superior government service from the Vocational Rehabilitation Administration, the Daniel T. Cloud Award for Leadership from CSUN, and the Distinguished Service Award from the NAD.

His professional activities in the service of others is equally impressive. A former president of the Gallaudet College Alumni Association, he also served his alma mater as a member of the Board of Directors and as Chairman of the Board of Fellows. Additionally, he was president of the Commission on Social Rehabilitation of the World Federation of the Deaf, Vice President of the Professional Rehabilitation Workers for the Adult Deaf, and a consultant to numerous organizations serving the Blind, the Deaf-Blind, and the Disabled.

To quote the words of Ralph Waldo Emerson: "An institution is the lengthened shadow of one man." For almost 40 years, Boyce Williams has been at the hub of the national rehabilitation movement in Washington, D.C. During this span of time, he has led the way in providing improved services to deaf and hearing impaired persons in the areas of health, education and welfare. Directly, and indirectly, his programs have also proved of benefit to persons with handicaps and disabilities throughout the world, and he has become a role model for deaf persons aspiring to leadership positions in all walks of life.

He was alone in the air, struggling with the controls of his little monoplane as it knifed through the blackening clouds. Every now and then, he felt the whole plane shudder as huge bolts of lightning exploded on both sides. The thought flashed across his mind: "To think that, only minutes ago, I left Kansas City with clear skies overhead. And now this—not one, but *two* electric storms!"

Somehow, he got through—"on a wing and a prayer," and using all the instructions he picked up in earning a pilot's license. He found a corridor of fairly quiet air between the two storms. Threading this needle, he maneuvered his single engined prop through the storm center and found daylight again. "Whew!" he grinned, patting the controls of his 65 horsepower Piper Cub. "We did it again—and without a land-to-air radio!"

Rhulin Thomas made history in 1947 when he became the first deaf pilot to fly an airplane alone from the Atlantic Coast to the Pacific Coast. This achievement seemed even more amazing than when Charles Lindbergh flew solo from California to New York 20 years earlier. Why? Because Rhulin Thomas was stone deaf and therefore unable to use any of the important land-air radio equipment a pilot normally uses and depends on.

Rhulin A. Thomas was born on a farm in Arkansas, July 29, 1910. A childhood illness left him totally deaf, after which his family moved and he went to the Missouri School for the Deaf for his education. Upon graduation, he attended Gallaudet College but withdrew after one year in order to support himself. He worked as a printer's apprentice for a while and then secured a job as a linotype operator for the *Washington Evening Star* newspaper. During his spare time, he took lessons in aviation and eventually received a pilot's license. After saving enough money, Thomas bought his own plane.

Soon afterwards, Thomas decided on his daring attempt to fly solo across the United States. He knew it could be dangerous. Unable to use the radio, he would have no way of knowing if he was approaching a bad storm until he was caught in it. The fear of the unknown, however, did not stop Rhulin Thomas. Besides, he had two good reasons for making the attempt. First, he wanted to prove that a deaf person could fly across the continent alone. Second, he hoped to reach California in time to greet two other aviators, George Truman and Cliff Evans, upon the return of their globe-circling flight. These men, both from Washington, D.C. had just accomplished a "first" by flying "tandem" around the world in two Piper Cub planes. And it was George Truman who had taught Rhulin Thomas how to fly at the Maryland Aviation School in 1946.

On October 26, 1947, Rhulin Thomas climbed into his Piper Cub and took off from Rehoboth Beach, Delaware. During his

3,000 mile flight, he experienced close encounters with terrifying storms in Indiana and Missouri. At one time, he lost his way during a storm and ran out of gas. His engine conked out and he had to make a forced landing on a farm. Often, his "flivver Plane" was buffeted by strong headwinds. When crossing Banning Pass, at 9,500 feet in the Rocky Mountains, he went on a "roller coaster ride" because of the down drafts on the other side of the mountains. Miraculously, he escaped this notorious "graveyard of pilots."

He finally sighted the Pacific on November 7 and touched down at Van Nuys Airport, Los Angeles. His timing was perfect, too, as he landed in time to greet Truman and Evans upon the completion of their own record-making flight. It was a historic event, later described in a *Colliers Magazine* article by Evans and Truman, who reported:

> There was a handsome crowd at the airport. Mayor Fletcher Bowron was there. The individual who gave our hearts the biggest lift, though, was a man you've never heard of. Rhulin Thomas is his name. A linotype operator in Washington, D.C., Thomas is both deaf and dumb. George taught him to fly in 1946 . . . Thomas had flown himself across the continent to meet us, and had nearly cracked up once en route. "Boys," he scrawled on his little pad, after we had shaken hands, "maybe your headlines weren't as big as Lindbergh's or Earhart's or Wiley Post's, but an awful lot of amateur pilots in the U.S.A. are awful proud of you."

George Truman was just as proud of Rhulin Thomas. And so were the deaf people of America who soon brought this pioneering achievement to the attention of the White House. Through the Missouri Association of the Deaf and the National Association of the Deaf, arrangements were made to cast a commemorative medal in honor of their daring deaf airman. On September 30, 1948, a special ceremony was held at the White House. Major General H. H. Vaughn, military aide to President Harry Truman, awarded Thomas with a gold medal

studded with three diamonds. On the back of the medal it said: "Rhulin Thomas—First Deaf Solo To Fly The Continent."

His pioneering achievement did more than to encourage other deaf persons to become pilots. It also let the whole postwar world know how proud this deaf hero was to be an American, in the land of the free and the brave. In accepting the medal, Rhulin Thomas said:

> "Thank you for this honor. I appreciate it and greatly appreciate, too, that the United States, our free nation, gives to the deaf equal opportunity to get not only education but higher education, licenses to fly airplanes and to drive cars, employment in the work of their choice, and all the rights and privileges of citizenship."

Shakespeare once said, "Actions speak louder than words." The deaf have understood the truth of that timeless proverb more than any other group perhaps. The truism also explains why sports have always been of special interest to the deaf.

While deaf persons may not follow the plot of an uncaptioned TV program as well as their hearing neighbors, they can equally enjoy and understand the "plot" of a televised football or baseball game, or for that matter, almost any sport. And when the camera zooms in for a close-up during one of those heated arguments between managers and umpires in a typical ball game, deaf viewers, if they can lipread, actually have an advantage over those hearing neighbors! The advantage applies in the stadium, too, if binoculars are used. (Remember the *Life Magazine* story about the deaf guy who lipread Queen Elizabeth at a football game?)

The fact that sports are synonymous with action also helps explain why many deaf youngsters become outstanding athletes. Sports provide shelter from the storm of spoken communication, and all the frustrations that may accompany it, for the average deaf youth. Unfortunately, as in many other things, opportunities for the deaf in organized sports are limited, especially after the 12th grade. Enter Art Kruger. An archetypal man-of-action since the 1930's, he has worked tirelessly at providing opportunities for the deaf to participate in and experience the thrill of national and international competition.

Art Kruger has been called the "guiding light," "founder," and "Father" of the American Athletic Association of the Deaf—the national athletic organization of the deaf founded in 1945 which has grown into a coast-to-coast empire with over 150 clubs. Kruger's dedication to the AAAD spans over 35 years, beginning as its founder and first president in 1945 and culminating in 1982, when he stepped down from his long-time position as chairman.

While he was guiding the AAAD all those years, Kruger was also spearheading the World Games for the Deaf U.S. Committee. He served as team director from 1957 to 1965, and then as WGD U.S. Committee chairman from 1966 to 1982, deservedly earning for himself recognition as "the heart and soul of the Deaf Olympic movement" in the United States. Too dedicated to the movement to step entirely out of the picture, Kruger assumed the position of Committee *chairman emeritus* in 1982.

Art Kruger is what some people would call a "self-made man." He is unafraid of challenges, of hard work, of trying as best he can to make his own fate. In short, he's a person interested in "doing," in "action." Yet, Kruger's efforts have always been not so much for himself, but for others, directed toward the ideal of enhancing the quality of life for the deaf everywhere, and encouraging deaf solidarity and pride.

Even in his younger years, Kruger was not content with sitting back and letting the world have its way with him. Fate had already done enough damage by deafening him when he was just three years old. Born in Philadelphia on March 6, 1911, Kruger enjoyed the normal life of a toddler until a fall from a burning apartment into a fireman's net somehow left him deaf.

He attended the Home for Training in Speech for Deaf Children in Bala, Pennsylvania, and various public schools. Later young Kruger went to the Mt. Airy School for the Deaf for one year, before enrolling at Gallaudet College in 1928. When he wasn't studying or making numerous friends in college, Kruger's attention was on sports—organizing, scheduling, recording and reporting Gallaudet's athletic activities.

Kruger's interest in sports in general, and in deaf sports in particular, made him an unknown authority on the subject. But his knowledge soon became public. When a well-known sports authority, Frederick Meagher, made his selections of the best basketball players in schools for the deaf in 1931 and published them in the *Deaf Mutes Journal*, Kruger wrote a letter to Meagher, complaining about some of the choices and making a few of his own. It was obvious to Meagher, the editors, and the readers of the *Journal* that Kruger knew his deaf sports well and was a real find. The letter opened up writing opportunities for Kruger. Eventually, he wrote for the *Journal* and other publications such as *The Silent Broadcaster* and *Deaf American*, selecting his own All-American deaf teams and chronicling the achievements of deaf athletes.

America, in 1932, was caught in the stranglehold of the Depression. Unemployment had become widespread; fear gripped everyone. Undaunted (and probably because he didn't have much else to do anyway), in the summer of '32 after his junior year, Kruger began a journey across America to see the splendor of the land and its melting pot of people. With a tattered travelbag in one hand and making the sign for the number "10" in the other, Kruger, like a deaf version of Woody Guthrie (low on money but high on enthusiasm) hitched rides all over the country and met all kinds of people, rich and poor. All were impressed by the young deaf man's sense of courage and fellowship.

With his thirst for travel quenched, the young journeyman returned to Gallaudet to start his senior year in the fall of '32 and continued to organize sporting events at the college.

Marriage, a job, and a home in New York followed Kruger's graduation from Gallaudet. And as the years rolled by, visions of an athletic organization of the deaf danced in his head. In 1938, Kruger began organizing national tournaments of schools for the deaf. Then he turned his attention to deaf clubs. With very little financial support, he put together a deaf club regional basketball tourney in New York City.

The Krugers moved to Akron, Ohio during World War II, and Art worked in the war plants. Although the war proved a tragedy, it ironically helped the deaf. America's deaf population found more jobs than ever during the war and were finally able to prove their worth to employers reluctant to hire them in the past. Akron, with its large manufacturing industry, became a sort of mecca.

As incomes improved, larger contributions to the clubs could be made by members. The growing treasuries provided the funds necessary for a national tournament. Such a dream became history on April 14, 1945, when the First National Club of the Deaf Basketball Tournament was held in Akron, with none other than Art Kruger as chairman. Teams from all over the country converged on the city, and Kruger was the magnet that brought them all together. The fact that the tourney happened in April seemed fitting. For April means spring— the season of birth. And the event at Akron marked the beginnings of the AAAD with, of course, Art Kruger as its founder and first president.

Almost single-handedly Kruger tackled the task of forging the AAAD into the fine-hammered steel-supported organization that it is today. The experience at Gallaudet helped him make decisions that required quick-thinking. Kruger drafted laws and procedures, and established a network of seven regional organizations. The AAAD served as the governing body for the seven regions. Rules and regulations were drawn in an effort to enhance the quality of play for both players and spectators. Participation in international deaf athletic competition also became a goal.

When the war ended, Kruger and his wife moved to Los Angeles where the "action" now was. There he began working at the Western Costume Corporation, the place he would eventually retire from, 30 years later, in 1975. At Western Costume, the largest costuming firm for the movie and television industries, Kruger headed the Materials Department. In his free-time, he continued to build the AAAD with imagination and dedication.

The World Games for the Deaf had been launched back in 1924 in Paris, when Kruger was only 13 years old. But because of lack of leadership, organization and funding, no representatives from America were sent until 1935. Even then, the number was small—only two U.S. athletes competed in the Games that year in London, England. But with Art Kruger at the helm, things would be different. And so, in 1957, with

Kruger as team director, forty deaf American athletes participated in the World Games in Milan, Italy. Actually they did more than just participate. The American contingent won 23 medals during the competition—seven were gold.

Kruger continued as team director for the 1961 Games, and for the 1965 Games in Washington, D.C. In 1966, the workhorse and founder of the AAAD became chairman of the WGD U.S. Committee, serving in that capacity up until 1982. All the while he worked laboriously at trying to collect the necessary funds to support U.S. Deaf Olympic teams. American Deaf Olympic athletes are sponsored or funded by private contributions from individuals and businesses, and the costs increase every year as teams grow and inflation rises.

Although there is no way to measure exactly how many hours Art Kruger put into fund-raising over the years, the amount of money he was able to raise should give some indication as to the degree of his hard work and dedication to the cause. Including the record $730,000 collected to send an assemblage of 213 athletes, coaches, and officials to the 1981 Games in Cologne, West Germany, Kruger has raised over $2,000,000 during his association with the WGD!

At the '81 Games in Cologne, the Americans placed 1st in collecting medals, a total of 111. Our deaf athletes from all over the country have been given the opportunity, through the help of people like Art Kruger, to show the nation and the world what they are made of and the level of excellence they can achieve.

Kruger's service to deaf athletics is unequalled and has been recognized by numerous organizations. In 1954, he was most fittingly elected to the AAAD Hall of Fame. The Helms Foundation Hall of Fame (Founded by a nephew of Bill Hoy, the deaf professional baseball player) honored Kruger with induction in 1973. At those 1981 Games in Cologne, the Comite International des Sports Sourds (CISS) awarded Kruger a gold medal for his "tireless and unselfish service to the deaf athletics." Other accolades include the Powrie V. Doctor Medallion for International Service and the Edward Miner Gallaudet International Award.

In 1982, Art Kruger received an Honorary Doctor of Pedagogy degree from Hofstra University during the May commencement ceremonies.

The list of awards bestowed upon Art Kruger is truly amazing, and too long to include in full. But to the man who built the AAAD, seeing that almost impossible dream of the 1930's materialize was probably award enough. The AAAD and the U.S. WGD committee are big "hits" now. They are still going strong. But the deaf community will never forget who wrote the script and directed the production. Art Kruger—the dreamweaver who made things happen by putting the emphasis on "Action."

To many hearing people, the telephone probably ranks as one of the greatest inventions of all time. Its development made communications over distance an easy and popular thing. Just pick up the phone, dial, talk and listen.

Alexander Graham Bell, the inventor of the telephone, was also a teacher of the deaf. He even dreamed of someday developing a visual device which would aid the deaf in communication. This never became a reality. Instead, he had to be content with the telephone which, ironically, put deaf people at a great disadvantage. Yet, he was not to blame. If Mr. Bell hadn't arrived at the patent office and submitted his patent application three hours before another telephone inventor, Elisha Gray, he never would have been credited with inventing the telephone. Gray would have. The point is that the telephone was destined to be invented by *someone.* It was just a matter of time.

Although Bell's intentions were good, the telephone became a major obstacle in the deaf person's crusade for social and economic equality. A deaf person could not call up a friend across town as could a hearing person, nor could he expect to be hired for any kind of job in which the use of the telephone was necessary.

But, in 1964, about 90 years after Bell's invention, a deaf man named Robert Weitbrecht introduced an invention of his own which is now helping the deaf put the telephone to useful work. His invention was an electronic device called an *acoustic coupler* or *terminal unit.* The acoustic coupler (TU) enables typewritten communication over the telephone through the use of a teletypewriter. Teletypewriters are communicating devices used by special agencies such as the military and Western Union. Weitbrecht's invention literally joined the teletypewriter and telephone together, resulting in what Weitbrecht is credited for inventing—the telephone-typewriter or "TTY."

By the end of 1982, there were over 150,000 TTY sets in the United States. They are not only located in deaf people's homes, but in many public places and businesses such as airline reservation desks, police departments, hospitals, and schools. Because of Weitbrecht's invention, deaf people now have moved one step closer towards equal enjoyment of the technological "luxuries" and necessities of modern culture.

Robert Weitbrecht was born deaf in Orange, California on April 11, 1920. Even when he was a small boy, he often wondered about different ways in which people could communicate with each other. As a teenager, he became interested in communication over distance and was an amateur radio operator licensed by the FCC (Federal Communication Commission). Because of his hearing-impairment, Weitbrecht used amplified Morse Code to communicate over the radio.

After completing public elementary and high schools, he attended the University of California (Berkeley) and graduated in 1942 with a degree in astronomy. It was still the period of World War II, and Weitbrecht chose to remain at Berkeley for the next three years where he was employed as a physicist. There was also another reason. It enabled him to work closely with the distinguished scientist, Professor Ernest O. Lawrence, director of the radiation laboratory at Berkeley and inventor of the cyclotron—the machine which first split the atom.

Weitbrecht then became an electronic scientist for the Aeromedical Laboratory at the University of California from 1945 to 1947, before going to the U.S. Naval Air Missile Test Center at Point Mugu, California, where he helped develop precision timing and number coding systems. During his four years there, Weitbrecht designed radar systems, electronic optical devices for cameras, and also developed the "WWV" Radio Time Signal used worldwide today.

From 1951 to 1957, he was a Research Associate at Yerkes Observatory, University of Chicago. While earning a M.S. degree in astronomy there, he helped develop photoelectric guiding systems and photoelectric photometers. Returning to California, he worked at the Stanford Research Institute's Communications Laboratory, 1958–1969. There, he designed a precision astrometric camera system for the Lick Observatory. It was the first electronically guided camera in the world. He also worked for NASA (National Aeronautics and Space Administration) on an earth satellite (ECHO) project.

Weitbrecht began working on the TU or acoustic coupling device in 1964, during his spare time, and completed work on it the same year.

The first public demonstration of experimental TU's was staged in June 1964 in the Hotel Utah, Salt Lake City, by the Communications Committee, Oral Deaf Adults Section, of the Alexander Graham Bell Association for the Deaf. After a year of continued development and testing via long distance telephone lines, using old Western Union machines, the R.H. Weitbrecht Company was formed to manufacture TU's. By 1967 Weitbrecht had acquired a patent and trademark, and the Applied Communications Company was formed to succeed R.H. Weitbrecht Company. Weitbrecht became Vice President and the company began manufacturing TU's, under the trademark "PHONETYPE". The next year, 25 TTY stations were in operation throughout the U.S.A. and American Telephone & Telegraph Company (AT&T) agreed to release surplus TTY's to the A.G. Bell Association through the Western Electric distributing houses of Bell telephone system affiliate companies.

The proliferation of TTY's soon followed with the organization of Teletypewriters for the Deaf, Inc. (TDI). It was spearheaded by two deaf leaders—Dr. H. Latham Breunig, its Executive Director (1968–1980) and past president of the Oral Deaf Adults Section of the A.G. Bell Association, and Dr. Jess M. Smith, past president of the NAD and editor of its national magazine, *The Deaf American.*

Swift advances in electronic technology have since led to a wide variety of telecommunication devices for the deaf. These sophisticated TTY's now employ computer or Baudot modem, television screen, digital read out—and some can combine digital read out with paper print out. Hence, the evolution of the term TDD, "Telecommunications Devices for the Deaf," which also resulted in the organizational change to Telecommunications for the Deaf, Incorporated.

With headquarters in Halex House, the home of the NAD, TDI is a non-profit organization serving a membership of over 100,000. It publishes a National Directory, listing names and addresses of TDD/TTY consumers, and also sends out a monthly newsletter, *GA-SK.*

All this the deaf have wrought since 1964—and it all began with Robert Weitbrecht's brilliant invention.

Weitbrecht, who also holds an honorary membership in Telephone Pioneers of America, has been an amateur radio "ham" (W6NRM) since 1936. In 1951 he petitioned the Federal Communications Commission (FCC) to open low frequency amateur radio bands to Radio Teletype. This resulted in FCC Docket No. 10073, which opened bands to Radio Teletype in 1953. Ever since then, he has been active in research and development of anti-fade systems for improved Radio Teletype reception.

For his development of Timing Systems at the U.S. Naval Air Missile Test Center (California), he was given an award for Superior Accomplishment in 1949. In 1969, he was one of ten nominees for Outstanding Handicapped American of the Year, and in 1974 Gallaudet College awarded him with the honorary degree of Doctor of Science for his outstanding work as a physicist and his great contributions to the deaf.

Dr. Weitbrecht is an avid outdoorsman who often goes hiking and camping in the California mountains. He also has a private pilot's license with a land airplane rating. In 1982, he was off and flying on a new business venture with the establishment of "Weitbrecht Communications, Inc.", based in San Carlos, California. As Chief Engineer, he continues refining TDD instruments and evaluating the sales product. Additionally, he developed a computerized Dial-A-News system, known as "Microdan," which now has five units in operation in the Los Angeles and San Francisco areas.

For him, it was just another link in the rapidly developing network of Telecommunications services. But for deaf America, it meant building better bridges of communication among themselves—and their "Open Sesame" to equal opportunity.

When the National Association of the Deaf was founded in 1880, none of its members dared to dream that its annual operating budget would someday approach two million dollars or that their Home Office would be located in a building of their own. Eighty four years later, it still seemed but wishful thinking. By 1980, however, these "castles in the air" became living realities with the joyous Centennial Celebration of the NAD in Cincinnati, Ohio, the place of its birth. Fittingly, the NAD Centennial was dedicated to the man who gave substance to such dreams—Frederick C. Schreiber.

At the time when he first took up the reins as its Executive Director in 1966, the NAD consisted of a few thousand members. With no home office of its own, the NAD had to function wherever its incumbent president resided. There was no paid or permanent office staff, all the work being done by volunteers and by its elected officers (all of whom had full time jobs elsewhere). Indeed, it was a wonder how the NAD had survived for so long and maintained its objectives of serving the general welfare of deaf Americans as their "watchdog" and advocate.

If the NAD expected to carry on this responsibility, it would certainly have to enlarge its membership, develop greater deaf awareness and consumer programs through dynamic outreach activities, and take on a corporate "Madison Avenue look" similar to contemporary human rights organizations.

This was the viewpoint of Fred Schreiber, who literally had to become a modern day Moses, as well as another Mahatma Gandhi, and convince his followers to believe in his visionary ideas and plans of action. Fortunately, like all great leaders in history, he was well-equipped to tackle this challenge. Not only did he possess the necessary backbone and idealism, but he also had spent most of his life rubbing elbows with deaf people from all walks of life—at school, at work, and at play.

Frederick Schreiber was born in Brooklyn, New York, on February 1, 1922. At the age of 6, he was stricken by spinal meningitis and became totally deaf. He attended the Lexington School for the Deaf and then transferred to the New York School for the Deaf because of a school policy requiring all boys to attend this "military-type" academy. At "Fanwood," as it was then nationally known, he learned the importance of discipline. He also picked up a knowledge of the printing trade, which he later put to good advantage in the working world.

He graduated at the age of 15 and became one of the youngest students enrolled in the Preparatory Class at Gallaudet College in the fall of 1937. Gallaudet opened new horizons to the "Kid from Brooklyn." There, he learned the art of persuasion from "soap box" debates; he took an active part in organizational activities which served to draw out his leadership potential; and he developed the service-oriented philosophy which was to last him a lifetime.

This was put into practice shortly after graduation from college in 1942. It was at the height of World War II and Schreiber did the next best thing that a handicapped American might do—he went to work in a war plant. As a machine operator at the Firestone Company in Akron, he helped produce vital materials and equipment for our men in front-line action. In doing so, he was not alone. There were thousands of other deaf persons who found ready employment in the Akron-based war industries. They came from all over the country and made a veritable "melting pot" of deaf Americans.

During his five years at Akron, Schreiber became most active in the cultural and community affairs of the deaf. He also learned much about politics at the local club and state association levels, gladly offering his services as committee man, officer, fund raiser, and in countless volunteer capacities.

When the war ended, he spent one year as a teacher at the Texas School for the Deaf, and then went home again, to New York City, where he joined the printer's union and worked as a linotype operator. In "the Big Apple," he was an active club member in the affairs of the Brooklyn Association of the Deaf where he removed the "sex barrier" that existed at the time and made regular membership accessible to women. He had married in 1944 and because of his growing family needs, he also "moonlighted" by working as a part-time tutor of illiterate and immigrant deaf clients at the New York Department of Vocational Rehabilitation.

These contacts not only brought him face to face with the "grass roots deaf" but also made him aware of the serious communicative disorders that existed among them. He became especially concerned about the rigid academic policy in many schools for the deaf which banned the use of sign language. This, he felt, hindered the educational development of many deaf students, especially in reading and writing, and was the cause of later unemployment problems after leaving school.

Believing that such problems deserved political action at the national level, Schreiber decided to become more actively involved with the NAD. His first move was to relocate himself and family to Washington, D.C., in 1952. He got a job as a printer for the *Washington Post* newspaper, where he worked for several years, and then became employed at the U.S. Government Printing Office. At the same time, he was making himself seen as well as heard at NAD conventions and other organizational meetings. Like a master tactician, he was also busy with his own leadership training program.

His first big step was to become Executive Director of the District of Columbia Club of the Deaf, which he revitalized into a model community center. Next, he improved communication channels with its membership. As founder and editor of their monthly publication, *Dee Cee Eyes*, he included news and opinions on major developments, problems and issues affecting the deaf population at large. His pet topic was the NAD, which he proposed should increase its membership by establishing a national network of state association affiliates. He also argued for a permanent base of operations in the nation's capital city, where the NAD could become a more effective lobbyist organization. He communicated these proposals so convincingly that, at the NAD Convention in 1964, he was unaminously elected Secretary-Treasurer.

His accomplishments thereafter bordered on the incredible.

In October, the NAD established headquarters in a downtown Washington office suite. He lobbied successfully with various federal agencies and obtained several grants which helped develop public awareness and enrich the NAD treasury. From the U.S. Office of Education, he won long-term contracts for the evaluation and selection of Captioned Films for the Deaf. From the Vocational Rehabilitation Administration, he secured a contract to start a continuing education program in Washington and establish sign language classes for interested hearing persons. A third grant was obtained from the Office of Economic Opportunity to evaluate the need of a Job Corps program for deaf youth.

Although he was doing all this voluntarily while holding down a full-time job as a printer, Schreiber was getting the message across. When the next NAD Convention was held in 1966, he was elected to the salaried position of full-time Executive Secretary. The catch to "the salaried position" was that it paid only half as much as he was making as a printer. However, he took the job and tackled the challenge.

Beginning with one secretary, he obtained a federal grant to hire more personnel so as to manage the business affairs of the newly-established Registry of Interpreters for the Deaf which the NAD helped organize. Other federal grants went to develop nation-wide programs for sign language classes and the establishment of a National Consortium of Programs Training Sign Language Instructors. To provide the basic textbooks needed for these purposes, the NAD became both bookseller and publisher. One of its most successful money-makers was the best-selling publication *A Basic Course in Manual Communication* (1973), compiled by Terrence J. O'Rourke, who also directed the nation-wide communicative skills program. Eventually, a whole range of books on the subject of deaf people and deafness was to be published by the NAD, and the book sales brought in big profits.

By 1968, the NAD had doubled the size of its home office, expanded the staff of paid employees and provided them with hospitalization and life insurance benefits. It had also obtained a large grant from the VRA to conduct a world conference, "The International Research Seminar on the Vocational and Educational Rehabilitation of Deaf Persons," held in Washington, D.C., which Schreiber planned and directed. An ever greater undertaking was initiated with the award of a grant to do a national census of the deaf. This exhaustive study was done by Jerome Schein and Marcus Delk and it was completed in 1974 under the title, *The Deaf Population of the United States,* published by the NAD.

Fred Schreiber received valuable assistance in many of these undertakings. It was to his credit, however, that he could listen to advice from the right persons and work in harmony with them. One of these, Dr. Jerome D. Schein, Director of New York University's Deafness Research and Training Center, was his chief consultant in grantsmanship. There were many others, deaf and hearing, whom Schreiber tapped, drafted, and buttonholed—all for the purpose of providing better services for deaf people through the NAD.

In 1971, the NAD purchased "Halex House," a two-story building in Silver Spring, Maryland, with 21,500 sq. feet costing $640,000. The staff was increased to 28 full-time and 11 part-time employees in 1972, and the following year Halex House was the scene of a gala dedication ceremony as deaf and hearing persons from far and near came to admire Fred Schreiber's masterwork.

The wisdom behind this acquisition soon became obvious. A large part of the mortgage could be paid off gradually through the profits from expanding activities and from rental of office spaces to other organizations. This was another of Fred's ideas—to provide a common home for major organizations of the deaf fighting for a common cause. It became a reality by 1982 when the following groups set up business in Halex House: National Registry of Interpreters for the Deaf; American Deafness and Rehabilitation Association; Telecommunications for the Deaf, Inc.; International Association of Parents of the Deaf; Inter-national Catholic Deaf Association; Convention of American Instructors of the Deaf; Conference of Educational Administrators Serving the Deaf.

By that time, too, the NAD employed 40 full-time workers. It had also ballooned so as to support a Branch Office in Indianapolis, a fully-owned research unit (Deaf Community Analysts, Inc.), and a Legal Defense Fund (the only legal action organization that serves the deaf community on a nation-wide basis). Unfortunately, all this exacted a toll from its "empire builder," Fred Schreiber, whose health began to fail in 1973 following a heart attack.

After recovering, however, he picked up his hectic pace. It included endless miles of travel throughout the United States and foreign countries—on NAD business or as its advocate of equal rights and opportunities for the deaf. He experienced several other serious illnesses but still carried on in a heroic gesture of defiance against physical limitations. Even at the thousand and one social functions and informal parties, "Freddie" could always be found—with a smile on his lips and a song in his heart. For he just loved to sing and sign, especially with a group of deaf songsters. These sing-a-longs in sign became his trademark wherever he traveled, and his "lifeline" from one stop to the next.

"Freddie" was only human, however, and his song came to an end on September 5, 1979. His friends arranged a special memorial service which was held at Gallaudet College. The college auditorium was filled to overflowing as friends and dignitaries came to pay homage to a great leader and humanitarian.

They praised his good deeds and dedication, and they cited the many honors that he had received. Chief among these were an Honorary Doctor of Laws degree from Gallaudet College; International Solidarity Medal, 1st Class, from the World Federation of the Deaf; Daniel T. Cloud Leadership Award from the National Center on Deafness, California State University at Northridge; Administrator's Award from the National Rehabilitation Association.

In 1981, the NAD published an excellent biography by Dr. Jerome D. Schein, *A Rose for Tomorrow: A Biography of Frederick C. Schreiber*. Another lasting tribute is by the deaf poet, Robert F. Panara, whose poem epitomizes the man and his achievement:

FREDERICK C. SCHREIBER

None had the vision such as he
  To plan and build, on faith alone,
Foundations for the N.A.D.,
  A home to call our very own.

He took the challenge and the charge;
  He found no task too great or small;
He "buttonholed" the deaf at large
  And made believers of us all.

He moved upon the world's great stage
  And won the hearts of small and great;
He caught the spirit of the age
  And urged them to communicate.

His goal, in every word and deed,
  Was but to leave a legacy
Of strength in union and in creed
  Embodied by the N.A.D.

These were the truths he would impart—
  To labor with a love divine;
To speak the language of the heart
  In tune with hands that sing and sign!

In 1979, a young woman was pushed off a crowded subway platform in downtown Manhattan during the evening rush hour. She fell into the tracks and one of her hands was sliced off by a subway car as she tried to roll away. Quick work by the police and a team of ambulance medics saved her life. They also recovered her hand, packed it in a bag of ice, and drove the woman to Bellevue Hospital where her hand was reattached to her wrist by method of microsurgery.

Microsurgery is a new kind of surgery done by specially trained doctors who use powerful microscopes while operating. In that young woman's case, it took two teams of surgeons 16 hours to reattach her hand—one team working on the stump of her arm and the other team with her severed hand. The chief surgeon was Dr. William W. Shaw, chief of the reconstructive plastic surgery service at Bellevue. The woman regained partial use of her hand, with the prospect that it may have almost normal function in the future.

The story, which was featured in the New York newspapers, had all the elements of a "soap opera" episode on television. Yet, "the story-behind-the-story" might have added to the human interest. Few people realized that it was a deaf person who had taught the technique of microsurgery to the chief surgeon. That person is Dr. Donald L. Ballantyne, Director of the Microsurgery Training Program at New York University Medical Center, who is also known as "the master teacher behind-the-scene."

Donald Ballantyne, Jr., was born in far away Peking, China, on November 8, 1922. His father, an American, was manager of an international bank in the Far East. His mother was Australian and they made their home in Hong Kong.

While still a baby, Ballantyne became ill from pneumonia and the high fever damaged his auditory nerves so that he became totally deaf. His mother was reluctant to place him in a school for the deaf in America to learn how to speak and lipread. Instead, she decided to teach him herself. She attended classes and read numerous books until she herself had mas-

tered the subject and was prepared to teach her son to speak and lipread.

Because of his father's business in China, the family was constantly on the move—shifting from Shanghai to Peking, then Hong Kong, Tientsin, and back again to Hong Kong. Often, they had to travel on antiquated Chinese junks crowded with coolie soldiers who had no consideration for foreigners. Once, on the Yangtze River, the Ballantynes had to lay flat on their backs on the deck of an old Japanese tugboat to escape the cross-fire of opposing Chinese and Japanese armies.

Because of the constant moving, young Ballantyne was enrolled in various schools—American, German, French, Italian. Not only did he manage to pick up some foreign words but he also somehow learned his "3R's." The key to getting this education was continual practice in speech and lipreading. Everyday, when he returned home from school, his mother was always there to improve his communication skills. Even the servants and coolies were required to talk to him all the time, using no gestures. Likewise, all his friends, and those of his parents. Talk! Talk! Talk! And, at night his father made him read aloud from newspapers and story books, always correcting his speech and pronunciation. To top it all, even his private tutors instructed their own children to correct young Donald's speech!

At the same time, the Ballantyne's didn't neglect their son's personal and physical development. To build up his strength, they saw to it that he learned to ride a bike, swim and sail a boat, go hiking and camping as a cub scout, and, later, to play a good game of soccer. When he also learned to drive a car, in his teens, Donald proved to be a mechanical wizard of sorts, as he was able to take apart his automobile engine and put it together again. This mechanical aptitude and nimble-fingered gift was to help him, later, when he developed an interest in microsurgery.

In 1936, when Ballantyne was 13 years old, his mother decided to send him to school in the United States since there was no higher education for American students in the Far East at that time. He was enrolled at Archmere Academy, a Catholic private school in Wilmington, Delaware, where he quickly showed that he could keep up with his normal hearing classmates academically. He also learned to play football, baseball and basketball for the first time.

Each summer, Ballantyne returned home to China alone, without a chaperone. Sometimes these long journeys from one continent to another proved to be quite exciting. Like the time, during the Sino-Japanese War in 1939, when he was returning to Archmere Academy on board the S.S. *President Hoover*, which was bombed by Chinese planes near Shanghai. The Chinese thought that his American ship was a Japanese troop ship.

It was all part of his "experiential education." It also helped him develop his self-confidence and self-discipline. The necessity of moving from place to place, or traveling thousands of miles alone, taught Ballantyne to find his way around, to meet strangers, to talk to and lipread people of different countries— on trains, aboard ships, and on land.

After three years at Archmere, he enrolled in the Canterbury Prep School, at New Milford, Conn., which had the reputation of high academic standards in preparing students for the best "Ivy League Colleges." He graduated in 1941 and was accepted as a freshman student at Princeton University. Not only was he the first deaf student admitted there but he also had the best test scores in German language of *any* student over the previous 25 years.

Ballantyne graduated from Princeton in 1945, after only three and a half years, with a B.S. Degree in Chemistry. He then went to Catholic University, Washington, D.C., where he received his Master's Degree in Chemistry in 1948, and his Ph.D. Degree in Biology in 1952. During that period, he also served as part-time Instructor in Biology at Gallaudet College, teaching deaf students. It was a busy period in his life, inasmuch as he not only learned another language, sign language,

by which to communicate with the deaf, but he also was courting a pretty young woman who had normal hearing. Her name was Mary Lou Milner and she was an undergraduate student at Duke University, which meant that Ballantyne did quite a bit of commuting in his Volkswagon between Washington and Durham, North Carolina.

They were married in 1952, shortly after their graduating ceremonies—he with a Ph.D. and she with a B.A. degree.

Dr. Ballantyne began his professional career as a research assistant in parasitology with Squibb Laboratories in New Brunswick, N.J. He then went to Chicago where he worked as a research assistant at the Illinois State Psychopathic Institute, investigating the effects of parasites in pregnant women who were being treated there. The laboratory testing was somewhat dangerous, and since his wife was expecting a baby then, he became fearful that he might carry home a contagious disease. Therefore, he was greatly relieved when he was asked by Dr. John Marquis Converse to join the Institute of Reconstructive Plastic Surgery at New York University Medical Center in 1954.

The invitation from Dr. Converse, a distinguished medical scientist, not only opened the door to an exciting new career in Experimental Surgery, but it also led to a most productive meeting of minds. Converse and Ballantyne went on to collaborate in writing scores of articles for scientific journals, as well as two books.

As a research associate in experimental surgery, Dr. Ballantyne began working in plastic surgery to heal victims of severe burns and wounds via transplantation of skin grafts. This involved transferring human skin tissue or organs from one part of the body to another. Soon, Ballantyne began doing countless experiments on laboratory rats which led to his discovery of a new method of transplanting human kidneys.

This came at the time that microsurgical techniques were first introduced in the United States during the 1960's. As more and more microscopes appeared in the operating rooms of large hospitals, it meant that there would be a great need to train doctors who were not used to working with the equipment and techniques. That is where Dr. Ballantyne helped fill in that need. As a pioneering researcher, he helped in the development of microsurgical techniques and became known as "a master teacher." Soon he became known internationally for his work in the regeneration of blood vessels in skin grafts and wounds; preservation of skin grafts by freezing and freeze-drying; and the use of silicone to correct deformities in the face and other areas of the body.

In all these, and related operations, surgeons use specially designed microscopes that magnify the operating field from 6 to 36 times actual size. The needle and suture thread are so small they can be used to sew human hairs together, end to end. The needle is so tiny that surgeons must use special instruments, instead of their hands, to handle it. A tiny artery, the size of a carpet thread, may need six stitches to reattach its severed ends. Using microscopes with foot-controlled "zoom" systems, surgeons can now reattach severed limbs and fingers, restore sight to eyes that are clouded by hemorrhaging, remove tumors, and redirect blood flow in the brain to save a stroke victim.

Dr. Ballantyne has taught Microsurgery at hospitals, universities, and research centers in many places of the United States and Europe. He has written and co-authored over 75 articles in medical journals and, with Dr. John Converse, he has written two books: *Experimental Skin Grafts and Transplantation Immunity* (1979) and *Microvascular Surgery: A Laboratory Manual* (1981).

He is a member of many scientific and medical organizations and he has also found time to be active in organizations serving the deaf. A charter member of the American Professional Society of the Deaf, he served as its president for many years; he has served on the New Jersey State Advisory Council on the

Deaf, and as a member of the Board of Trustees for the St. Francis de Sales School for the Deaf in Brooklyn, N.Y.

Dr. Ballantyne was the first to receive the *Amos Kendall Award* from Gallaudet College (1979), which is presented to a deaf person for notable excellence in a professional field not related to deafness. In 1981, he was honored by the National Technical Institute for the Deaf in Rochester, N.Y., when he was named the *Edmund Lyon Memorial Lecturer*, which introduces students from NTID and Rochester Institute of Technology to the life experiences of profoundly deaf persons who have distinguished themselves in various professions. It was fitting that such an outstanding medical scientist as Dr. Donald Ballantyne was the first recipient of this award at NTID, which offers deaf students a variety of career programs in medical technology.

LIBERIA

GHANA

NIGERIA

⊙ IBADAN

AFRICA

Throughout the course of history, black persons have played a major role in shaping the destiny of America. They have left their imprint in every walk of life—as political and spiritual leaders, intellectuals and artists, educators and scientists, athletes and entertainers. Who can forget such names as Frederick Douglass, Booker T. Washington, Jackie Robinson, and Martin Luther King? As freedom fighters and cultural carriers, these men gave new meaning to the American promise of "life, liberty, and the pursuit of happiness."

If these four men were alive today, they would certainly be impressed by the achievement of another black American, named Andrew Jackson Foster. Not only because of his "track" record" as a civil rights advocate, an educator, and a spiritual leader but also because of his heroic struggle to overcome the handicap of deafness and break "the color line."

The son of a coal miner, Andrew Foster was born on June 27, 1925, in Birmingham, Alabama. While attending public school in the suburban steel mill town of Fairfield, he was stricken with spinal meningitis at the age of eleven and became totally deaf.

After attending the Alabama School for Colored Deaf in Talladega, he moved to Detroit, Michigan at the age of seventeen. This was during World War II, and Foster participated in the war effort by working long hours in various factories that produced military equipment. At the same time, he tried to further his education by attending night school and taking correspondence courses at home. Two years after the war ended, he renewed his quest for an education while still working in auto factories. His diligence paid off when he received a Diploma in Accountancy and Business Administration from the Detroit Institute of Commerce in 1950, and a High School Diploma in 1951 from the American School in Chicago for his correspondence work at home.

In 1951, at the age of 26, Foster made history by becoming the first black deaf person to gain entrance to Gallaudet College in Washington, D.C. It was the first of many future "break-throughs" and pioneering achievements by this determined and dedicated young man. As the only black student, he literally found himself in a "fishbowl," with the eyes of all Gallaudet, as well as all America, watching his behavior and progress. But he proved to be equal to the challenge. Not only did he walk tall and proud, like a noble African chieftain, but he also had a handsome smile and a lively sense of humor that easily won friends and influenced people.

He impressed just as many others with his intelligence and stamina. By taking extra summer course work at Hampton Institute in Virginia, Foster managed to obtain the degree of B.A. in Education in just three years. He became the first black graduate of Gallaudet College in June 1954.

These three years in Washington were the turning point in his life. In his spare time, he would often go to the inner city or "ghetto" neighborhoods where he tried to locate other black persons who were also deaf. While working to help rehabilitate these people, Foster learned that, in all of Africa, there were only 12 schools for the deaf. He thus began to "have a dream" about bringing the light of knowledge of those unknown numbers of black deaf children "in darkest Africa." He also felt the spiritual calling to bring the message of Christianity to deaf Africans.

Discarding his earlier thoughts about a business career, he devoted full time to education and missionary studies. He earned his M.A. in Education from Eastern Michigan University in 1955 and, one year later, he received his degree in Christian missions from Seattle Pacific College.

In 1956, with the help of interested friends and church groups, Foster organized the Christian Mission for Deaf Africans, which was based in Detroit at that time. Under its sponsorship, he embarked on his one man crusade to carry education and the Gospel to the neglected deaf of Africa, an estimated number of 250,000 people. This was years before President John F. Kennedy later conceived the idea of "the Peace Corps."

With an unshaken faith and the shining vision of his "dream" to guide him, Foster arrived in Accra, Ghana, in 1957. After months of hard work, he located 53 deaf persons and set up a makeshift program in a rented Presbyterian public school building. Classes for children met from 4 to 5 in the afternoon, and for adults from 6 to 7 in the evening. In doing so, he had to perform many different tasks and roles—as teacher, evangelist, administrator, and public relations specialist. It was the kind of test equal to "the labors of Hercules," and Foster proved he had the expertise, the stamina and the patience to prevail. The two pilot programs developed into the Ghana Mission School for Deaf Children and the Ghana Mission Center for Deaf Youths and Adults, both of which were approved and nationalized by the government.

Inspired by this breakthrough and by his success in obtaining trained teachers of the deaf, Foster set off to explore new frontiers. In the country of Nigeria, he founded and directed three more Christian Mission Schools for the Deaf—at Ibadan (1960), at Kaduna (1962), and at Enugu (1962).

As destiny would have it, he met a remarkable deaf woman, Bertha Zuther, who shared his interest and zeal for missionary work. They were married in 1961, and together they devised a master plan to launch a chain of satellite schools and programs for the deaf in Africa. As co-founders, they opened up schools in Abidjan (Ivory Coast); Lome (Togo); Moundou (Chad); Dakar (Senegal); Cotonou (Benin); Bangul (Central Africa Empire); Kumba (Cameroon); and the African Bible College for the Deaf.

For each of these schools, Foster was chosen to serve as a member of the Board of Governors. In 1965, he was honored for his pioneering achievements by being elected President of the Council for the Education and Welfare of the Deaf in Africa. This multi-national cabinet was the first of its kind in all of Africa.

In 1970, Foster made a memorable visit to Washington, D.C., where his "dream" began. This was the occasion when his "Alma Mater," Gallaudet College, recognized him as the first

black deaf person to receive the degree of Doctor of Humane Letters, *honoris causa*, at its Commencement ceremonies. It also took great pride in citing Foster as a model for those black Africans, deaf and hearing, who had studied at Gallaudet and later returned to their homeland to assist in the education and rehabilitation of the deaf.

Similar recognition came from the Alumni of the colleges he attended. In 1975, he received the Gallaudet College Alumni Association Award "for promoting the well-being of deaf people of the world"; in 1980, he was named an "Outstanding Alumnus" at the homecoming activities of Eastern Michigan University; and in the same year he was runner-up in selecting the "Alumnus of the Year" at Seattle Pacific University.

In spite of the cultural, political, and economic problems that hinder progress in "The Third World" today, Andrew Foster's crusade goes on. With his devoted wife, Bertha, and their five children, he lives in Ibadan, Nigeria, where he still dreams of the day when "all God's children" will be *barrier free at last!*

WASHINGTON, D.C.

OFFICE OF EDUCATION

CAPTIONED FILMS FOR THE DEAF

STATE OF INDIANA

INDIANAPOLIS

When Al Jolson appeared as *The Jazz Singer* on the silver screen in October, 1927, and his voice was heard simultaneously on the sound track, it was like "the shot heard 'round the world." It set off a chain reaction which produced dramatic changes in the film industry and its repercussions were felt by many segments of society—for better or for worse. In particular, the shock wave dealt a damaging blow to deaf and hearing impaired people. Their silent films had suddenly "gone with the wind." In place, they were stuck with the new captionless "talkies" which deprived them of a major source of entertainment and information.

For almost two generations, thereafter, this communication barrier became a great "wall of silence" which isolated deaf people from the mainstream of society, culturally and educationally. They were also isolated within the family circle by not being able to understand and enjoy television programs. In 1959, however, their advocates and friends, both the deaf and the hearing, lobbied successfully for corrective legislation which led to an Act of Congress (PL 89-905) authorizing the establishment of Captioned Films for the Deaf.

From its humble beginning as an agency in the U.S. Office of Education—Department of Health, Education and Welfare—Captioned Films for the Deaf greatly expanded in size and function during the next 20 years. Its title changed from Media Services and Captioned Films (1970) to Captioned Films and Telecommunications for the Deaf (1975) to reflect the variety of media services it provided—from educational films and filmstrips to popular television programs. In 1981, their captioned services were further expanded so as to include the needs of other handicapped groups in the areas of special education. Known today as Media for the Handicapped, this special agency is directed by a special person who has been deaf since childhood, Dr. Malcolm J. Norwood.

Dr. Norwood has worked with all types of captioned media from the time he joined the agency in 1960. He has been in the forefront of almost every research and development program related to captioned media for the deaf, and he is the first deaf person to head a major program in the U.S. Office of Education. That occurred in 1970, when he was elevated to the position of Branch Chief of Media Services and Captioned Films for the Deaf. Soon afterwards, he was the first to envision the possibilities of closed-captioned television and his persistent efforts in this direction led to the present state of the art enjoyed by hearing impaired audiences.

"Mac" Norwood, as he is known to his friends and associates, was destined to do great deeds. The story of his life begins in the city and birthplace of educational opportunities for the deaf in America. He was born in Hartford, Connecticut, on March 16, 1927. At the age of five, he lost his hearing as the result of back to back cases of scarlet fever and measles. Like most hearing parents of deaf children, his mother was unaware that there were such facilities as schools for the deaf, so he was enrolled in a public school. This was somewhat ironic because one of the best schools for the deaf existed in nearby West Hartford—the American School, founded more than a century before.

For the first five grades in various public schools, Mac Norwood experienced a full share of problems and frustrations. Fortunately, a school nurse (whom he calls his "Irish angel") visited his mother one evening and urged her to send him to the American School for the Deaf. It turned out to be the best of all possible worlds as he came face to face with the rich heritage of the past, begun by Laurent Clerc. The art of sign language came to Mac Norwood as naturally as an Irishman takes to song. His self-image grew, along with the realization that there was no limit to what a deaf person can accomplish in life. To prove this, he graduated with honors at the age of sixteen.

He went to Gallaudet College in search of "new worlds to conquer." On his "royal road to romance," he discovered the books by Richard Halliburton which contained exciting tales of travel and adventure in far off places. As a means of preparing himself for such future journeys, Mac joined the varsity track and cross country teams. He also became editor of the college newspaper in his senior year and had a sign-singing role in the Drama Club's performance of *The Mikado*,—the closest he could get to geisha girls and Japan!

After graduating from Gallaudet in 1949, Norwood's itinerary began as a teacher in the Texas School for the Deaf. The following year, he returned to the American School for the Deaf where he taught for the next two years. He also fell in love with one of his students, a girl who shared his interest in reading the travel adventures of Richard Halliburton. They were married in 1952 and Norwood accepted a position at the West Virginia School for the Deaf as Director of Curriculum and Supervising Teacher of the high school program.

Always interested in visual aids for instructing deaf students, Norwood built up a collection of captioned filmstrips at the West Virginia School. He also established a budget to encourage his teachers to rent old-time silent films with captions for use in their classes. During summer vacation months, Norwood attended classes at the University of Hartford, receiving his master's degree in Education in 1957.

When Captioned Films for the Deaf was established in 1959, the person chosen to direct this federal agency was Dr. John A. Gough, who had previously served as Director of the Graduate School of Education at Gallaudet College. An experienced educator of the deaf, as well a former business man, Dr. Gough had also directed the teacher training program at Gallaudet. Some of these prospective teachers had been farmed out for practicum training at the West Virginia School, which was how Gough came to know about Malcolm Norwood and his interest in visual media for the deaf. In 1960, Gough made Mac an offer he just couldn't refuse, and he became the first deaf person to work for Captioned Films as a Program Specialist. He proved to be so resourceful and innovative that he soon became Gough's "right hand man."

As the saying goes, "A picture is worth a thousand words,"

and captioned media caught on so quickly that it became the "in-thing" for teachers of the deaf. It also held forth the promise of becoming the most popular form of entertainment for deaf children and adults.

For the first five years, its annual budget of $85,000 was mostly used to lease and caption Hollywood feature films. These were made available on free loan to schools for the deaf and other registered groups of deaf people, much like library materials. At a nominal cost, the price of return postage, a captioned film could be enjoyed regularly each week. As the acquisition of new films increased, so did the number of registered consumers. It was necessary, of course, for someone to own a 16mm. sound projector, an item which then became a sort of "status symbol" in the deaf community. This, in turn, fostered a renewed sense of "family" or community spirit which found expression in a variety of social customs. "Movie clubs" sprang up all over the country as friends got together to watch the Saturday night feature film. Often they were preceded by "pot luck dinners" or else followed by a lively critique and discussion. The same thing happened at the social functions of civic and religious organizations of the deaf.

In 1965, an amendment to the law (PL 89-258) provided CFD with an annual budget of $3 million and the opportunity to promote deaf awareness through outreach activities, as well as initiate research. Materials and services also became available to parents of deaf children, to social and rehabilitation workers with the deaf, and to employers of hearing impaired persons. It also had the means to loan out much-needed educational materials. These included films for teaching sign language and fingerspelling, lipreading and "Cued Speech," and even records for auditory training.

A network of over 50 depositories was set up across the nation to distribute materials. Most of these were in schools for the deaf, with each depository serving the area around it. Three major distribution centers in New York, Indiana, and Colorado (with deaf persons as managers) circulated the Hollywood entertainment films. Eventually, with the advent of computer technology, these functions became centralized and replaced by one major distribution center. Now located in Indianapolis, its employees are mostly deaf persons.

With Gough and Norwood leading the way, along with an expanding staff and a long chain of outside professional consultants, there seemed to be no limit to CFD's innovative programs. Among these was the training of teachers of the deaf in the use of new media at summer institutes established at the universities of Nebraska, Massachusetts, and Tennessee. Annual six-week workshops were also held at various schools for the deaf where teachers evaluated and selected educational films to be captioned, with a lesson guide for each film. To top it all, an in-service training program based at the New Mexico Foundation in Las Cruces, operated a "travelling road show" which gave demonstrations and short courses at schools for the deaf throughout the West.

While realizing "all this, and heaven, too," Mac Norwood was doing lots of traveling himself. He became so good at it, and at doing his own thing, that when John Gough retired in 1970, Norwood took over full responsibility of the programs. By 1975, it had magnified into Captioned Films and Telecommunications for the Deaf, and he had already pioneered the breakthrough into closed-captioned television programming. Somehow, too, he found the time to pursue doctoral studies at the University of Maryland. Upon the successful completion of his dissertation comparing hearing impaired viewer's comprehension of captioned and signed newscasts, he received his Ph.D. degree in 1976.

It was Dr. Norwood who had previously encouraged experimentation toward the development of a device or instrument that would enable captions to be broadcast but only seen by viewers with TV sets equipped with a special decoder. Through a joint undertaking by his Office, the Public Broadcast Service, and the National Bureau of Standards, the decoder was developed by NBS and called the "NBS TV Time System." It made possible a simple, inexpensive method of broadcasting captioned TV for the deaf.

After years of further development, testing, and evaluation this captioning device was eventually mass-produced for home use. The decoder was lightweight and portable, and it attached easily to any television set to display closed captioned programs. Also available for purchase was a color television set with a built-in decoding device, called a Telecaption set.

Leaving no stoned unturned, Norwood had already arranged for the establishment and funding of the National Captioning Institute (NCI) which would provide the actual captioning process. Permission to do so had already been granted in December, 1976, when the Federal Communications Commission granted authority to PBS and other broadcasters to televise closed-captions for the millions of hearing impaired viewers in the U.S. A non-profit organization based in Falls Church, Virginia, NCI now captions most of the materials presently being broadcast. Participating members are the Corporation for Public Broadcasting (CPB), ABC and NBC, and in some cases, individual stations and producers such as WGBH-TV of Boston. Revenues to cover the first several years of operating costs have come from these groups, along with funding from Norwood's agency and private corporations and foundations. Eventually, captioning should become a self-supporting operation.

At NCI, five caption editors work as a team in a row of fourteen specially equipped editing booths, taking around 20 hours to caption a half-hour TV program. The cost of captioning a one hour program is about $2,000. This is a "drop in the bucket" when compared to the cost of $250,000 for producing the average one hour TV program.

By 1983, over 70,000 telecaption decoders were purchased and being used in homes, schools, libraries—with an average number of 3.5 viewers per set. It represented an average audience of 250,000—which was only the beginning. Like the introduction of color TV in the late 1950's, as more captioned programming becomes available the number of telecaption sets and decoders purchased, as well as the total audience, will multiply.

Already, too, foreign countries have expressed a keen interest in closed-captioned television. They have often invited Norwood to explain and demonstrate its applicability, and this arrangement has proved mutually satisfying. It has given Mac the opportunity to travel to some of the places he read about in Halliburton's books!

At the same time, he has done his share in contributing his time and expertise to other programs and organizations of the deaf. In 1972, Norwood was asked to serve as liaison officer between the Bureau of Education for the Handicapped and the newly established National Technical Institute for the Deaf in Rochester, New York. He has served on the advisory committee of several schools for the deaf, the Maryland Association of the Deaf, and the State Advisory Board for Mental Hygiene for the Hearing Impaired in Maryland. His honors and awards include the Distinguished Service Award from DHEW in 1976; Special Service Award from the International Association of Parents of Deaf Children in 1980; President's Award from Gallaudet College Alumni Association in 1980; and the Certificate of National Recognition from the Association for Special Education in 1982.

Although he will often attribute his success to his "Irish luck," there's no doubt that Mac Norwood pulled his own weight in climbing to the top of the ladder. Yet, there was a time, in his first year at college, when it looked like he picked the wrong ladder to climb. That happened on a balmy night in April when, acting on "an Irish lark," he climbed to the top of the Chapel Tower and turned the hands of the huge Tower Clock one hour *backwards*. For this, he was suspended from college for *one year*.

In 1972, however, Gallaudet College awarded him with the Honorary degree of Doctor of Laws at its graduation excercises. Fittingly, his citation included both an "official pardon" and a touch of Irish banter: ". . . Although as a student, Malcolm J. Norwood, '49, turned the Tower Clock back one hour, he is forgiven. He has been turning time forward ever since."

In the world of theatre of the deaf, he is known as "B B." He has a background in show business that spans nearly four decades and his list of credits is long enough to fill a whole page in the *Players Directory*. Like Marcel Marceau, his identity is so personalized that almost everyone in the theatre knows what the initials "B.B." stand for—Bernard Bragg!

The deaf son of deaf parents, Bernard Bragg was born in Brooklyn, N.Y., on September 27, 1928. His first experience with the world of "make-believe" came from the influence and examples of his father, Wolf Bragg, a talented actor who founded a deaf amateur theatrical group when there was no deaf professional theatre at the time.

Almost from the day his education began, Bernard Bragg attracted attention. His good looks, intelligence and creative imagination set him apart as a born leader. At the New York School for the Deaf (White Plains, N.Y.), he helped establish the Dramatics Club and played the leading role in many of its productions. Even on his day of graduation in 1947, he held the center stage with his eloquent "Valedictory Address" and rendition of "The Star Spangled Banner" in dramatic sign language.

His mastery of expression continued to cast a spell over everyone during his student years at Gallaudet College. He dominated the stage as no one had ever done before and became known as "the Barrymore of college drama" as the result of his performance in the title roles of *The Miser*, *The Merchant Gentleman*, and *Tartuffe*. These achievements made him a two time winner of "Best Actor of the Year Award."

After graduating from college, Bragg accepted an offer to become a teacher at the California School for the Deaf in Berkeley. Always the "go-getter" as well as the "work-horse," he found time to get his master's degree in Education at San Francisco State College as well as direct the school dramatics program and participate actively in the Bay City's deaf community theatre.

In 1956, Bragg got the big break needed to capitalize on his talents. While performing in a San Francisco night club, he was seen by the famed French mime, Marcel Marceau, who invited Bragg to study with him in Paris. After spending the summer studying mime in Paris, Bragg returned to his teaching job at Berkeley. However, he soon began giving one-man shows in night clubs, gradually working up to such famous spots as "The Backstage," "the hungry i," and "The Outside-Inside" in San Francisco. In the first half of these shows, Bragg would present his regular rehearsed act in the traditional make-up of painted face, striped shirt and black pantaloons (a la Marcel Marceau). After intermission, however, he offered a bonus attraction that was wholly his own invention. He challenged the audience to test his creative ability by asking him to mime anything that came to mind—"A Hole-in-One," "King Kong Meets Marilyn Monroe," "Superman versus Popeye," "A One-Armed Wall Paper Hanger," or "A Man in A Public Rent

Toilet"! In these improvised skits, Bragg proved to be such a daring and skillful showman that people started calling him "the Houdini of Pantomime."

In 1960, Bragg became the first deaf person to perform regularly on television when KQED-TV in San Francisco hired him to do a weekly show. Billed as "The Quiet Man," he improvised mimo-dramas suggested by telephone calls and letters from TV viewers. Many of them were children and teenagers who thrilled to see their favorite tales retold without words by "The Quiet Man," who acted out all the parts himself—from Dickens' *A Christmas Carol* to Shakespeare's *Hamlet.*

When the National Theatre of the Deaf was organized in 1966, Bernard Bragg became a founding member and the first deaf person invited to join the Company. He was also the only deaf person with professional experience in the theatre, and everyone benefited from his leadership and guidance. During the next ten years, he gave himself tirelessly and unselfishly to whatever task he was asked to do. As an actor, he played the leading or supporting role in every production that went on tour in America or abroad. As an adapter, he translated into sign language many of the plays and poems performed by the Company. Above all, he helped develop the unique art form of visual expression, known as "sign-mime," which became the Company's trademark and added a new dimension of communication in the theatre.

Soon, the whole world took note of his achievements, and "B B" made every effort to satisfy the many foreign places which invited him to conduct workshops or perform on stage and television as a guest artist. One of his most memorable experiences occurred in 1973 when he visited Russia under an exchange agreement of deaf actors and spent four weeks with the Moscow Theatre of Mimicry and Gesture. His performance as "Hermes" in the Aeschylus tragedy, *Prometheus Bound,* won such applause from the Russian audience that, when the play was over, the whole cast of characters on stage raised their thumbs in his direction—a universal gesture of acclaim.

This event was later featured in *Soviet Life* (Feb. 1975) which also said that only one other American had ever performed with Russians, and that was the famed black actor, Frederick Aldridge, who had done so over 100 years before.

It has often been said that, for Bernard Bragg, "all the world's a stage." He proved it again, several years later, when he was granted a sabbatical leave by the NTD Company to undertake a world tour. It was sponsored collectively by the NAD, the U.S. Department of State, the Ford Foundation, the International Theatre Institute, and the NTD. From September of 1977 to February, 1978, he covered 38 cities in 25 foreign lands, visiting deaf theatre companies and communities. He encouraged their creative development and shared with them the theatrical language developed by the National Theatre of the Deaf. In particular, he showed them the art of "sign-mime" and made them aware of its potential to become the universal language of deaf theatre.

Upon returning to the U.S., Bragg was invited to become a guest artist in residence at the National Technical Institute for the Deaf, in Rochester, N.Y., where he played the leading role in the NTID production of Moliere's classic comedy, *The Would-be-Gentleman.* Several repeat performances were presented afterwards when the NAD held its biennial Convention at Rochester, in July, 1978.

Bragg ended his long association with the National Theatre of the Deaf in September of that year to accept a position on the professional staff at Gallaudet College. In addition to lecturing on theatre and drama, he conducted workshops at various colleges and communities having theatre programs for the deaf. In 1979, he wrote and directed a one act romantic comedy, *That Makes Two of Us,* in which the eternal conflict, "oralism vs. sign language," is happily resolved by Cupid and kisses. The next year, he collaborated with Dr. Eugene Bergman of Gallaudet College in writing a major play, *Tales from A Clubroom,* which reflects deaf community life through the mirror of its Saturday night socials at the local club. Directed by Bragg, it was the feature presentation at the Centennial Convention of the NAD, July, 1980, in Cincinnati.

Like Bob Hope, America's ageless showman and good-will ambassador, Bernard Bragg continues to entertain audiences and promote the cultivation of theatre by and for the deaf. The publication of a biography of his life, *Signs of Silence* (1972) by Helen Powers, is a lasting inspiration for aspiring deaf Thespians to aim for the stars.

CHICAGO DAILY

10¢

EXTRA!
DEAF LAWYER DEFENDS
DUMMY LANG IN TRIAL

In 1979, CBS Television presented a two-hour dramatization of a true story which happened in Chicago, Illinois, in 1965. It was based on the best-selling book, *Dummy* (1974), by Ernest Tidyman, who also wrote the TV version. The program was about Donald Lang, a young black deaf-mute accused of murder, and the efforts of a deaf lawyer, Lowell Myers, to defend and help the accused deaf man.

Lowell Myers was one of the very few deaf lawyers in the United States, and the judge who presided over the case thought he would be the best person to represent Lang in court. Lang could not speak or lipread, nor did he know how to write or communicate in sign language, so he could not explain at the time of his arrest what had happened. It was the beginning of one of the strangest trials in legal history.

Lowell Myers proved to be a brilliant lawyer whose dedication matched his compassion. He firmly believed that Lang had been unjustly accused and he tried to prove that Lang was the victim of a chain of circumstantial evidence. The case made the front pages of the Chicago newspapers, and in May, 1970, it went to the Illinois Supreme Court. Finally, in February of 1971 the charges against Donald Lang were dropped and he was freed.

Unfortunately, six months later Lang was accused of another murder. It was almost a carbon copy of the first case. Once again Lang was convicted, mostly on grounds of circumstantial evidence, and Lowell Myers was called to defend Lang. Although Lang was found guilty, the decision was reversed on appeal, in 1975, because he was unable to communicate and defend himself. Lang was put in a state hospital where it was hoped that a special educational program would help him develop the communication skills which are necessary for him to defend himself when he is ready to stand retrial.

Donald Lang was only one of the thousands of deaf people that Lowell Myers has defended and helped throughout the years. Myers, who is also a Certified Public Accountant, has devoted his law practice towards serving the deaf and making sure they receive the same rights as hearing people.

Early in his career, Myers realized the vital need for having interpreters in courtroom situations involving deaf persons. He proved that point by personal example in the Donald Lang case. Even though his speech and lipreading skills are exceptional, Myers employed an oral interpreter who sat facing him, silently repeating the words spoken by the various participants in the courtroom scene. This was his own sister, Jean Myers Markin, who also knows sign language. She functioned as the skilled assistant he required in courtrooms and related situations.

With Myers' help, the legal system became more aware of the problems and needs of the deaf. He drafted the first comprehensive statute to provide for interpreters for the deaf in Illinois whenever deaf persons were arrested or questioned by the law. This legislation became mandatory in Illinois, and it has now been copied by half of the states in the nation.

Lowell Myers was born to deaf parents on January 26, 1930, in Los Angeles, California. His hearing was defective at birth and thereafter it gradually worsened. At the age of 12, his condition was diagnosed as "nerve deafness," probably inherited, and he experienced almost total deafness. By that time, the family had moved to Chicago where his father was employed as a printer.

After attending grammar school, Myers went to Lake View High in Chicago, also a public school for the hearing. He then progressed rapidly in pursuit of a career in business. From Roosevelt University, he received a B.S. degree in Business and Accounting in 1951, and one year later he graduated from the University of Chicago with the degree of MBA in Business Administration. Shortly afterwards, he became a Certified Public Accountant.

Although Myers was successful in his work as an accountant, he felt something was lacking. That was "the personal touch," the desire to work more closely with people. More specifically, he felt the urge to help people who were handicapped, especially in cases involving the law, and not just straighten out tax accounts. These handicapped persons were deaf, like himself, and others were deaf-mutes. There were untold thousands of such people living in Chicago whom he felt could benefit greatly by having the services of a lawyer who could communicate with them directly—in their own language.

In 1952, Myers applied for admission to the John Marshall Law School. Some of the school administrators were reluctant to permit him to attend. They felt that it would be impossible for him, because of his deafness, to succeed in law school. Others, however, were willing to take the risk and believed he should have the opportunity to try. Four years later, Myers graduated with honors, ranking second in his class, and received the degree of J.D. in Law. In the same year, 1956, he was admitted to the Illinois Bar and was licensed to practice law.

He did it the hard way, too. He worked as an accountant by day, supporting himself and paying his tuition, and at night he attended classes. Moreover, he went through law school without the assistance of an interpreter.

Upon graduation from John Marshall, Myers got a job with Sears, Roebuck & Co. as a tax auditor. On the side, he set up a practice as attorney-at-law for deaf clients. He was the only lawyer in Illinois who could make a practice out of defending and serving the deaf. By this time, too, Myers had married and was ready to start a family.

As his reputation grew, so did his law practice, which also included hearing people. His success in handling the legal matters of the deaf was largely due to his ability to relate to their special needs and problems, and to his skill in relaying these difficulties to the judges and juries in the courtroom. He also had a soft spot in his heart and found it difficult to turn down deaf people. He knew that if he didn't help them, there would be no other lawyer with the ability to communicate with them.

For this reason, he often accepted token fees from those deaf persons unable to pay more. Take the Donald Lang Case for example. When it was made known that Lang had no funds to pay a defense lawyer, Myers accepted the case immediately because he knew what would happen to Lang if he did not. As it turned out, Myers received one thousand dollars from the State for his defense of Lang, or an average fee of $2.00 per hour.

As the saying goes, "When the going gets tough, the tough get going." This fits the image of Lowell Myers. A tireless crusader for the rights of the deaf, he is also regarded as being rough and relentless whenever the occasion demands. This truth is emphasized in Ernest Tidyman's book, *Dummy*, which presents a vivid account of Myers' ongoing battles in support of equal legislation for the deaf.

One memorable example is the time when Myers fought for the passage of a law in Illinois that would allow deaf persons to drive automobiles. The resulting scenario, as Tidyman describes it, was full of dramatic irony:

> "When the legislation appeared to be bottled up in committee because of the 'disability' of the deaf, Myers investigated the committee members for disability. He discovered that four members were alcoholics, three myopic beyond the legal limit for car drivers, one helplessly crippled by arthritis—all holding licenses to drive. Myers wrote to each of these lawmakers of his own findings, with carbon copies to their colleagues."

Needless to say, Myers was victorious. To quote his own words, "The legislation was voted out of committee and approved at what I would guess to be 90 miles an hour."

Not content with trying to pass laws and making them stick, Myers has also written several books on the subject of deaf interaction with the law. In 1967, he published *The Law and the Deaf*, which was a professional edition for judges and lawyers who have since found it a valuable resource. Now in its 4th printing, the book is also valued as a training manual for persons interested in becoming professional workers with the deaf in interpreting and rehabilitation services.

Myers later wrote another version of this book which could be understood by young deaf readers. It also provides a wealth of information about the legal problems deaf students might encounter upon enrollment in school. This Student's Edition, now in its 8th printing, has proved so popular that it is used in English speaking countries throughout the world.

Lowell Myers may well be called "the deaf legal advocate of the deaf." A role model for present and future deaf lawyers, he is also greatly esteemed by his normal hearing peers and colleagues. In 1979, he was honored with the award of "Distinguished Alumnus" by the John Marshall Law School at a banquet attended by 700 people.

Today, Lowell Myers maintains a wholesome equilibrium in dividing his time between his law practice and working as a tax attorney for a large national corporation. Although he no longer works as a CPA, he is still adept at "balancing the scales." His present law practice is split 50–50 in the service of deaf and hearing clients. And he still tells it like it is: "My clients like me and my opponents dislike me—which is just the way it should be!"

In recent years, many loyal sports fans in America have complained that professional sports just aren't what they used to be. Some say the spirit of the game has been lost, that athletes these days are more like businessmen. Fans contend that player strikes and skyrocketing salaries may someday destroy everything. Others, however, argue that ball players deserve to be well paid for their "productivity."

But no matter what anyone thinks, one thing's for sure: As long as baseballs, footballs and basketballs are made, and as long as there are places to play, there will always be kids and adults who will perform and watch just for the sheer fun of it and out of a true love for the game.

Bill Schyman is one such person. Since his childhood, Schyman has had a never-ending love affair with basketball—an affair he was able to turn into a career. Deaf since birth, Bill Schyman made his way from neighborhood courts and school teams, through three fabulous years with the mighty varsity team at DePaul University, into the prestigious ranks of the National Basketball Association (NBA). He was the first deaf athlete to play big time college varsity basketball and to play professionally.

In addition to a brief season with the NBA Baltimore Bullets, Schyman played for the Washington Generals and the Boston Whirlwinds—two teams that traveled around the world with the razzle-dazzling Harlem Globetrotters performing as their opponents. Schyman also played for the Philadelphia Spas in the old Eastern Professional League.

Schyman's career with the Bullets was short because, soon after he joined the team, they folded due to financial difficulties. It was at this point that he connected with the Whirlwinds and later the Generals. He played with them for three years. After he tired of traveling and quit pro ball. Schyman's love affair with the game didn't end. He joined deaf basketball teams, leading them to three national championships. He also played for and coached Deaf Olympic teams, besides coaching at Gallaudet for five years. In 1979, Schyman's dedication and con-

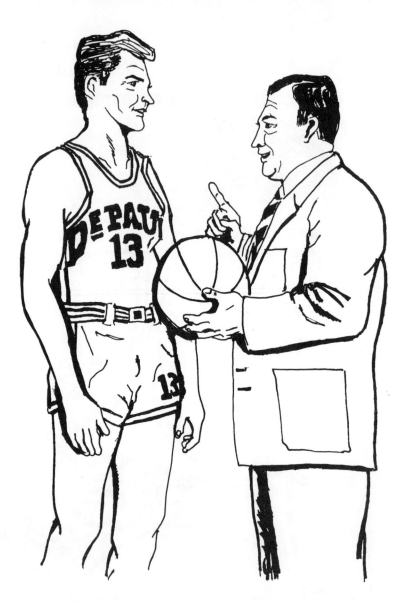

tributions to the game were recognized when he was admitted into the American Athletic Association of the Deaf (AAAD) Hall of Fame.

Bill Schyman was born deaf on February 14, 1930 in the windy city of Chicago. His parents, unaware that there were any schools for the deaf in the state, sent him to public school. By the time Bill was twelve, he towered above most of the other kids around—kids who didn't particularly care to be his friends because he spoke "differently." But once they noticed what a basketball player Schyman was becoming, they were quick to make him the "center" of attention, asking him to join in their pick-up games.

As a youngster, Schyman was a basketball fanatic, spending all of his time after school and on weekends at the b-ball courts. Not even hunger pains could stop him from playing, so his parents had to bring his lunch to him many times. Schyman went to Lane Tech High School in Chicago, but was unable to make the varsity team until his junior year, during which time he played occasionally as a sub. But as a senior, Schyman broke into the starting line-up with a bang, helping his team to a winning season and the playoffs by scoring a team-high average of 29 points a game.

His basketball prowess that year, 1949, attracted the college scouts. Four colleges—DePaul, Loyola, Notre Dame and the University of Illinois—offered him scholarships. Schyman picked DePaul because he liked Chicago and because he didn't want to miss any of his mother's home cooking!

Schyman never regretted choosing DePaul because it was there that he met Ray Meyer, the famous coach of DePaul's basketball team, and the man most responsible for developing Schyman into a first-rate basketball player. Meyer emphasized tough defense and strong re-bounding skills—intimidation "under the boards." Meyer forced Schyman to work constantly at sharpening his game to perfection. After an undefeated season his first year at DePaul with the freshman team, Schyman moved into Meyer's awesome varsity team and became the only sophomore that year to make the starting line-up. Schyman's aggressiveness under the boards, along with his 6'5" 200 lb. frame, quickly earned him the nickname of "Moose" and the reputation of "most feared player" on the DePaul "Blue Demons" team.

The "Blue Demons" played all their home games at the 20,000 seat Chicago Stadium. Schyman was always in the spotlight because of his unique situation—he was the first deaf player to make it as a starter on a top-contending college varsity basketball team. Although Schyman's deafness didn't prevent him from becoming a star with the Blue Demons, it did cause some difficulties. Like the game against Oklahoma. With ten seconds remaining and Oklahoma leading by only one point, Schyman, thinking that time had expired, handed the rebound he had just wrestled away from his opponents to the referee. That was a tough one to lose. But mix-ups like that were rare.

All in all, Schyman enjoyed three outstanding varsity years with DePaul. In his junior year, he was named "Most Exciting Player" by the Chicago newspapers. And during his senior year, DePaul enjoyed one of its finest seasons, placing in the top twenty week after week. At the Christmas Holiday Tournament in New York City, against unbeaten and number one ranked LaSalle at a sold-out Madison Square Garden, Schyman and the "Blue Demons" stunned everyone by upsetting LaSalle. And at the re-match in February, DePaul beat LaSalle again as Schyman scored fourteen points and muscled down twenty rebounds. LaSalle's record that 1952–53 season was 26–2. DePaul had played the part of "spoiler" to what would have been a perfect year for LaSalle. The "Blue Demons" themselves placed third that year in the NCAA playoffs.

The Baltimore Bullets drafted Schyman during his senior year at DePaul. He was eager to sign the contract but waited until he returned from the Maccabiah Games in Israel, where, as captain, Schyman led his USA team to a gold medal victory. Signing the contract before going to the Games would have resulted in a loss of amateur status and disqualification from the Games. So, after returning from Israel and graduating from DePaul with a B.S. degree in psychology, Bill Schyman joined the Baltimore Bullets of the NBA in 1953 and became the first deaf player to make it to the "big leagues" of basketball. Unfortunately, before the season was even a month old, the financially shaky Baltimore franchise folded.

But Schyman's pro career was saved when the owner of the world-renowned Harlem Globetrotters gave Schyman a position with the Boston Whirlwinds—the pro team that was touring with the Globetrotters. Playing with the Whirlwinds, and later with the Washington Generals, Schyman enjoyed traveling to countries such as Canada, France, England, Ireland and Israel. He always played against the same team—those exciting and comical Harlem Globetrotters.

Tiring of the extensive travel required as a Globetrotter opponent, Schyman retired from professional sports after three years and went back to Chicago where he worked for IBM. But it wasn't long before he was back on the courts, this time with the AAAD club. Joining the deaf club was the first experience Schyman had with other deaf people; he had always been "mainstreamed." As would be expected, the skilled veteran of the pros led his Chicago team, and later, deaf teams from Washington and Buffalo, to AAAD championships.

In 1962, while he was practicing in Washington with the Chicago deaf team in preparation for the Deaf Olympics in Finland, Schyman was offered a coaching position at Gallaudet College. He accepted and coached the 1962–63 Gallaudet team to its first winning season in over fifty years. Schyman coached at Gallaudet for five years and earned a master's degree in Education at American University before accepting a teaching position at a Maryland high school.

Some of Bill Schyman's other accomplishments include coaching the 1965 USA basketball team to a gold medal in the World Games for the Deaf in Washington, D.C., and coaching the 1981 USA team to a gold medal during the Deaf Olympics in Cologne, Germany. He also referees varsity high school basketball games and owns and operates the "Pine Lake Camp for the Deaf" in the Poconos, a summer camp of sports instruction.

Schyman's induction into the AAAD Hall of Fame in 1979 seemed a fitting tribute to a man who has contributed and accomplished so much out of an honest love of sports.

Schyman, in an effort to show just how important basketball has been to him throughout his life, asked in his will that he be buried with a brand new basketball tucked under his arm. He also said in a lecture that he hopes he can bring that ball with him when he reaches those "pearly gates." There's no doubt that if he *is* able to sneak the ball past heaven's door, the first thing Bill Schyman will do is pluck that heavenly halo from atop his head and turn it into a heavenly hoop!

At the age of one, Eugene Hairston became deaf from a battle against spinal meningitis. Twenty-one years later, in 1951, he was considered by many boxing experts and fans to be one of the few middleweights around with a chance of beating the great Sugar Ray Robinson for the World's Middleweight Championship.

Eugene Hairston was the most successful American deaf boxer in the history of amateur and professional boxing. As an amateur, the black youth compiled a stunning record of 60 wins and only 1 loss. As a professional, his record was an impressive 45 wins (24 by knockout), 13 losses, and 5 draws.

During his professional boxing career (1947–1953), Eugene "Silent" Hairston fought many of the leading middleweight contenders of the world. Some of the more famous boxers he fought were Kid Gavilan, Bobo Olson, Jake La Motta, Johnny Bratton, Paul Pender and Paddy Young. Hairston did very well against many of these top contenders. On October 30, 1950, he defeated Kid Gavilan in a ten round bout. Gavilan later became the 1951 welterweight champion of the world. In another contest, Hairston beat Paddy Young on a TKO (technical knockout) after just two rounds. And on April 30, 1951, Hairston, "the quiet kid from Bronx, N.Y.," KO'd Paul Pender, the man who later became the 1960 and '62 middleweight champ.

Hairston was a crowd-pleaser because of his aggressive and hard-hitting style of boxing. *Ring Magazine* (May, 1948) had a story about him, entitled "New Faces," which described Eugene "Silent" Hairston as a young fighter "with a devastating right and better-than-average boxing ability who should make the grade." By 1951, Hairston indeed had shown everyone that he could "make the grade." In its April issue that year, *Ring Magazine* listed him as the 2nd leading middleweight contender in the world!

The story of Eugene Hairston is a tale of determination. If not for his will power, he never would have become a boxer. Some people thought that, because of his deafness, the odds were heavily against him. But Eugene proved them all wrong.

Eugene Hairston was born in Harlem, N.Y.C., on July 23, 1930. He was educated at Public School 47, a day school for the deaf in Manhattan. His father, a house painter, had hopes that Eugene would become an artist because the young lad had shown a real talent for drawing in P.S. 47. However, Gene's boyhood idol was the great black fighter, Joe Louis, and he often dreamt about becoming a boxer. Little did his father know that, someday, Eugene would become a great boxing artist!

Gene had to quit school at the age of 15 to help support his brothers and sisters. After working at various jobs such as parking cars and pin-spotting in bowling alleys, Gene decided to turn his dream into a reality. One day in 1945, he showed up at a gym in the Bronx known as the "Tremont Athletic Club"—the place where fighters trained. Having arrived before the place opened, Gene decided to wait for the owners to arrive. When they finally showed up, Hairston quickly handed them a piece of paper with the words, *"I want to fight."* Then he performed a fast and furious shadow boxing routine. The owners were skeptical. They refused to allow the deaf kid to practice at the gym. This, however, didn't discourage the ambitious youth. Every day, for six months, he enacted the ritual of waiting at the club for the owners to arrive and then shadow boxing for them when they appeared.

Gene's persistence paid off. The owners finally agreed to let him box a few rounds with some amateurs. Hairston looked so strong and impressive in the ring (he outlasted four opponents) that the owners, Mike and Joe Miele, decided to give him a chance. Mike became Gene's manager and Joe his trainer. The two Italian brothers were just what Hairston needed. Their communication system combined "body language" and speech. They would gesticulate instructions to him between rounds and supplement this with well-formed words which Hairston lip-read. It was the beginning of a winning team.

Young Eugene, guided by the expertise of the two Miele brothers, quickly made his mark in the amateur boxing ranks.

In 1947, he captured two prestigious titles: New York Golden Gloves Champion, 137 lb. Open Division; and Chicago Intercity Golden Gloves (147 lb.) Welterweight Champion. After 61 amateur bouts, Hairston had lost only one!

The Miele brothers, realizing the great potential Eugene possessed, wasted no time. In the summer of '47, they entered him into the professional ranks. Now it was Hairston's turn to waste no time. Amazingly, the young deaf rookie won his first 16 professional fights—the first four by knockouts!

Everyone began noticing Eugene Hairston. *Ring Magazine* called him "The Deaf Wonder." *Ebony Magazine* gave him star billing in a feature story and called him "the only fighter with a chance against the now-legendary Sugar Ray Robinson." Fans applauded his courage and determination, while network television began broadcasting his fights—he appeared 13 times on national TV. Eugene "Silent" Hairston was making himself heard and was on the march.

He was also changing the scene of the boxing ring. Because Gene couldn't hear the time-keeper's bell which rang out the end of a round, the Boxing Commission of New York installed flashing lights on each of the 4 ring posts in the Madison Square Garden. When the lights flashed on, Hairston knew it signaled the end of a round. It also helped hearing boxers who often couldn't hear the bell ring because of noisy crowds. These flashing lights were also installed on the ring posts of many other arenas, and today they are widely used as standard ring equipment.

Unlike many boxers who favor one hand, Hairston was a hard hitter with both fists. But he did have a favorite punch and that was the "one-two," left jab and right cross. His ability to hit hard enabled him to tire an opponent with constant body punches. Then, when the opponent let down his guard, Hairston would attack with that "one-two" combination.

By the time "The Deaf Wonder" fought former middleweight champ, Jake La Motta, on March 5, 1952, he had fought in 58 fights and lost only 10. *Ring Magazine* had been ranking

Hairston as one of the top middleweight contenders for two straight years.

The confrontation with La Motta was a dramatic one. The setting was a sold out 10,000 seat Olympia Stadium in Detroit, with national TV exposure. Jake La Motta, who was known as the "Bronx Bull," was desperately in need of a victory. He had lost his middleweight crown to Sugar Ray Robinson eighteen months before and had been doing poorly ever since that loss. The critics said he was "washed-up," finished. La Motta promised his father that if he lost the fight to Hairston, he would quit.

The sentimental choice with the crowd was La Motta. They didn't want to see him quit, so they were cheering for him to win. "The Deaf Wonder" couldn't hear those cheers for La Motta when the ex-champ's name was announced, but Eugene surely must have felt the pressure. Added to his stress was the fact that he would have to win if he hoped to get a chance at fighting Robinson for the title belt.

So, the stage was set. Careers were on the line. The young, rising Eugene "Silent" Hairston vs. the old, fading and perhaps finished Jake La Motta. The ropes around the ring weren't the only things that were taut in Olympia Stadium that night.

Eugene followed his manager's advice throughout the fight by trying to wear down La Motta with body punches. And, when the opportunity came, Gene would employ his old favorite, the one-two combination. He landed quite a few of them during the bout, which was a "slam-bang" battle from start to finish. It was to Hairston's credit that he had La Motta reeling a few times. Nobody had ever knocked out La Motta, and nobody ever knocked "the Bronx Bull" off his feet—before or after.

The fight went the full ten rounds. Although the referee awarded the win to Hairston, the two judges ruled it a *draw*. Under Michigan rules, it was called a draw by split decision.

But Jake La Motta never forgot that fight. He mentioned his bout against "Silent" Hairston in his best-selling book, *Raging Bull*, which also became a major motion picture.

"Silent" Hairston never got the chance to fight Sugar Ray Robinson, nor did he ever realize his dream of becoming a champion. Fate stepped in to deal him an unlucky blow. The draw with La Motta gave Robinson the option of defending his title against Bobo Olson. Hairston, in a last-ditch attempt at getting a match with Robinson, challenged Olson to a bout. The fight was held on August 27, 1952, but Hairston lost on a TKO. He suffered severe damage to his right eye and later experienced blurred vision. Because the injury was a serious one, the New York State Athletic Commission suspended Hairston's boxing license. Soon other states followed the New York ruling.

Refusing to throw in the towel, Hairston went to Paris, where he fought against European middleweight champion Charley Humez. But after losing a ten-round decision, and unsuccessfully trying to get his license reinstated, Hairston knew it was time to quit.

When Hairston hung up his gloves in 1953, he left the ring like a man of class. Not once in his career had he ever asked for special rules because of his handicap, nor was he ever involved in any "fixes" or scandals of the kind that have hurt the reputation of many boxers. As the first black deaf prizefighter, he left a record that has a special place in the annals of boxing. The name of "Silent" Hairston will always "ring a bell" with his former opponents, and with the millions of people who saw him perform in the ring and on national television.

A great favorite with deaf fight fans, he received many ovations and honors from his own people. Among these was a black marble statue which read: "Eugene Silent Hairston, 1951 Welterweight Contender. From the Scranton Association of the Deaf." In 1975, he was feted at a huge luncheon and received a handsome plaque commemorating his induction into the American Athletic Association of the Deaf "Hall of Fame." And in 1983 he was the guest of honor at the Annual Banquet of the NTID Student Congress, National Technical Institute for the Deaf, where his life story was the subject of a special television program produced at NTID.

PLAYBILL

LONGACRE THEATRE

CHILDREN OF
A LESSER GOD

It was a Sunday night in June, 1980. The Mark Hellenger Theatre on Broadway was filled to overflowing by those who had come to attend the annual Antoinette (Tony) Perry Awards program. The audience included hundreds of celebrities from the entertainment world—and the unseen millions of other people who were watching the nationally televised CBS-TV spectacle. The special attraction, as everyone knew, would be the presentations honoring the best performers and the best play of the new season of plays on Broadway.

Finally, the time came for the grand climax and a hushed silence fell over the entire audience. The presenter opened the first envelope, drew out the vote, and exclaimed: "And the winner for the best performance by an actress is . . . Phyllis Frelich . . . for *Children of A Lesser God!*"

The odds against such a personal triumph seemed almost astronomical at the time when Phyllis Frelich was born on February 29, 1944. She was the oldest of nine children, all deaf from birth, and her parents were also deaf. Her girlhood home was a small farmhouse in Devil's Lake, North Dakota, and life was hard for the growing family who had few luxuries. There were other and more lasting qualities, however, which enriched the family and molded their character. There was joy and laughter and good-natured teasing—all expressed in their native American Sign Language. Little Phyllis was especially gifted and would often entertain the family and neighbors with "make-believe" roles and skits in dramatic mime and sign.

It was at the North Dakota School for the Deaf where Phyllis received her education. After graduating, she enrolled in Gallaudet College, where she majored in Library Science. However, her first love was dramatics, and she took an active part in many plays. Her outstanding performances as *Medea*, and as the Leader of the Chorus in *Iphigenia in Aulis*, won her the award as best actress of the year.

The "Summer of '67" proved to be an unforgettable experience and the turning point in her life. Shortly after graduating from college, she was invited to join the National Theatre of the Deaf, in Waterford, Conn., as one of its founding members. It was there that she met Robert Steinberg, a young man with normal hearing who became the stage manager for the professional company. During the courtship that followed, Phyllis taught Bob sign language, and a year later they were married.

The next phase of her life was devoted to motherhood and family. Two boys were born to the Steinbergs, named Reuben and Joshua. Both children had normal hearing and both learned to communicate in sign language, the first born actually learning to sign before he spoke his first words.

During this period, Phyllis followed her husband's career interests in the theatre. First came a stay in Oklahoma City, where Bob worked as resident designer for the Mummer's Theatre. They then moved to the University of Rhode Island, where he assumed a faculty position in the theatre department. The move allowed Phyllis to rejoin the NTD in nearby Waterford, Conn., and she performed with the company during the next two years. It may have also set the stage for the big breakthrough she later made on Broadway.

The chain of events began when Phyllis met the playwright, Mark Medoff, during the time she was a guest actress at the University of Rhode Island and he was guest playwright. Medoff had already written a successful play, *When You Comin' Back, Red Ryder?*, and now was intrigued with the idea of doing a play about the problems of the deaf in a hearing world. The more he talked with Phyllis and her husband, the more determined he became to write such a play. To prepare himself for this, he even learned to communicate in sign language.

In January, 1980, Medoff invited Phyllis and Bob to his home in Las Cruces, New Mexico, where he served as chairman of the theatre department of the State University. Gradually, the play began to take shape as Medoff found new insights into "the deaf experience," including the deaf versus hearing experiences of the married couple. Often, Phyllis and Bob improvised scenes for the play, which is a fictional story about the romance between a speech therapist and a deaf woman student. Their later marriage problems are the result of communication breakdowns and her active involvement in deaf rights. Their difficulties, however, have a universal appeal as each explores their individual need for independence. The play includes two other deaf characters in minor roles who also help provide a better understanding of deafness and deaf people.

When the script of the play was finally completed, Medoff gave it the title, *Children of A Lesser God.* It was first presented in a workshop at the State University with Phyllis as the deaf student, "Sarah Norman," and Bob as "James Leeds," the speech therapist.

Shortly afterwards, the play was brought to Los Angeles by Gordon Davidson, the artistic director of the Mark Taper Theatre. Under his brilliant direction, the play moved swiftly through the preliminary auditions, call-ups, and rehearsals. The leading male role of "James Leeds" was taken over by John Rubinstein, the rising young star of stage and screen. It was a demanding role, as Rubinstein had to communicate in fluent signs with Frelich and at the same time speak her half of the dialogue. The setting of the play also challenged the imagination of the audience. To emphasize "the silent world" of the deaf, there was very little scenery, and even the props were mimed.

The result was that *Children of A Lesser God* caught on like wildfire. After a successful run in Los Angeles, it opened on Broadway, March 30, 1980, at the Longacre Theatre. Its impact was so great that it won the acclaim of audiences and critics. "Tony Awards," the highest honor in the theatre, went to it as "Best Play," and for "Best Actress" (Phyllis Frelich) and "Best Actor" (John Rubinstein). The Outer Critics Circle named it "the most distinguished new play" and they hailed Frelich's acting as "an outstanding debut."

In the months that followed, the play performed to packed houses and the demand for tickets continued to build up. To meet this demand, another company was formed to take the

FOR BROADWAY'S BEST ACTRESS IN **CHILDREN OF A LESSER GOD**

play on tour. This was the National Tour Company which appeared in major cities throughout the U.S. and Canada. Soon, two other groups were added. The "Bus and Truck Company" played in smaller cities of the U.S., and the "London Company" traveled abroad to England where it enjoyed a long run. In each of these touring companies, a deaf actress played the role of "Sarah Norman." By 1983, over 20 deaf persons had been employed in leading or supporting roles, and as understudies.

Phyllis Frelich continued to perform on Broadway in the original production of *Children of A Lesser God,* which ran continuously for over 2 years. She also won many honors and made special appearances on television in response to the increasing demand for her services.

She was honored by her native state of North Dakota when Gov. Allen Olson presented her with the "Theodore Roosevelt Rough Rider Award" in 1981. In the same year, she was featured with Hal Linden on NBC-TV in a *Barney Miller* episode in which she played a deaf prostitute with sexy realism and humor. And in March, 1982, she participated in the ABC-TV spectacle, *Night of 100 Stars,* for the benefit of the Actors Fund of America.

On that *Night of 100 Stars,* she joined an exclusive group of celebrities from stage, screen and television. It was the most visible proof that Phyllis Frelich has now become a star of the first magnitude in the world of theatre.

"That's Linda!" Children shout delightedly whenever the pert and pretty brunette shows up on their television screen. Her little admirers may not realize that Linda Bove is the first deaf person to perform on *Sesame Street*, the popular daytime program of the Children's Television Workshop (PBS), but they all know who she is. Their eyes follow her every movement and facial expression as she helps them learn the vocabulary lesson of the day. One child says "house" in English; another pronounces the Spanish term, "casa"; and then Linda's hands will shape the word and paint its picture in the air.

Her act is so successful that she is often seen in *Sesame Street Magazine*, which features color photographs of Linda making the signs for words or fingerspelling the ABC's of the manual alphabet. By communicating with hands that talk, she helps children become aware of our multi-cultured society and also shows them how the deaf can contribute to the world of entertainment and education.

Sign language came natural to Linda from the day she was born to deaf parents, November 30, 1945, in Garfield, N.J. She received her early education at the St. Joseph's School for the Deaf in New York City, after which she transferred to the Marie Katzenbach School for the Deaf in Trenton, N.J.

After graduating in 1963, she went to Gallaudet College, where she majored in Library Science. Her real interest, however, was in the theatre. During her last two years, she was highly praised for her performances as "Polly Peachum" in *The Three Penny Opera* and as the female lead in *Spoon River Anthology*. This led to an invitation, after graduating in 1968, to join the National Theatre of the Deaf.

While with the NTD, Linda fell in love with Edmund Waterstreet, a classmate of hers in college who had also joined the Company after graduation. Together, they went on national tours and helped develop the matchless ensemble acting for which the NTD has become famous. Their marriage, two years later, made them the first deaf husband-wife team with any professional theatre group.

Since 1968, Linda has performed in leading and supporting roles in many of the Company's repertory of plays. Among her major triumphs were *The Love of Don Perlimplin and Belissa in the Garden* and *Priscilla, Princess of Power.* As "Priscilla," the girl who turns into Wonder Woman, she "wowed" everyone with her melodramatic acting in this hilarious drama of pop-art and comic strip, which was directed by Edmund Waterstreet.

Bove has always been ready, willing and able to lend her talents to other areas of theatre. As one of the five Company members who started The Little Theatre of the Deaf, a branch of its parent troupe, she has directed and starred in many of its productions. "LTD," as it is affectionately called, has brought delight and wonder to children of all ages, races, and creeds. After its Christmas Week success in 1972, *The New York Times* called it "the most rewarding kid's show in town!"

In 1973, Bove successfully auditioned for the role of "Melissa," a deaf character, for the longest-running CBS serial, *Search For Tomorrow.* The story line involved a young deaf girl who is employed as a library cleaning woman in the hospital where she just recovered from an auto accident. Although she is deaf, "Melissa" is aware of her right to live her own life, and she has run away from over-protective parents. She is taken in as a foster daughter into the home of one of the leading characters in the serial, who learns to read "Melissa's" signs as well as the deaf girl reads her lips. "Melissa" meets a young doctor who can communicate in sign language because his mother is deaf. They fall in love . . . and eventually marry.

Although it was typical of "soap opera," the story of "Melissa" portrayed some of the problems deaf persons have in the world. For a period of 25 weeks, Linda captured the hearts of millions of TV viewers. She also helped greatly to break down barriers of misunderstanding and to enhance the social image of the deaf.

Linda Bove is still blazing new pathways for the deaf on prime time television. In 1974, along with Marlo Thomas, she received the AMITA (Italian-American) Award for her outstanding work on television. In 1976, she signed a long term contract as a permanent resident of *Sesame Street*. In February, 1980, Linda became the envy of every young woman when she was cast with Henry Winkler on *Happy Days*, ABC-TV's popular serial. As "Fonzie's" deaf girlfriend, Linda Bove not only won his heart but also made him declare his love in sign language!

Indeed, her beauty and personality are such that she is everybody's sweetheart. She is also very photogenic. These qualities, along with her talent, have yielded many spinoff benefits. She has helped provide employment opportunities in television programs for other deaf women. She has also made sign language become a most visible and popular medium of communication. Many members of *Sesame Street* and *Search For Tomorrow*, as well as the crew of TV technicians, have learned sign language from Linda. And, in 1980, *Sesame Street* and the National Theatre of the Deaf cooperated in publishing a book, *Sign Language Fun With Linda Bove*. Illustrated by Tom Cooke and featuring Jim Henson's lovable "Sesame Street Muppets," the book offered a highly visual approach to educating children by method of body language and "talking hands." Thus, too, children could benefit from the book without having to watch the television show, and the revenues from the book sales were used to help support Children's Television Workshop Programs.

Her impact on living theatre is no less dramatic. During 1980–1982, Bove contributed greatly to the long-running stage hit, *Children of A Lesser God*, in the role of the deaf heroine, "Sara Norman." In the original Broadway production, she was indispensable as the understudy and stand-in for her NTD colleague, Tony Award winner Phyllis Frelich. And when the National Tour Company was formed, Linda was billed as the star attraction in major theatres throughout the United States and Canada.

Covering a wide range of interests in theatre and communications, Linda Bove has gradually established herself as the

foremost deaf woman in the performing arts. Her work has become internationally known, and although she now acts mostly as a consultant to NTD, she has become their leading ambassadress.

In the Fall of 1979, Bove played a major role in NTD's world tour which covered 30,000 miles. The brainchild of its founder and artistic director, David Hays, who also wrote the major production, *The Wooden Boy*, the repertory also featured Linda as "Mrs. Webb" in Thornton Wilder's *Our Town*. She also directed a companion piece, *The Four Fables*, by James Thurber, and had a role in *The Tale of the Magic Painter*, which was directed by her husband, Edmund Waterstreet.

The highpoint of the tour was the visit to Japan, which had been arranged in advance by Tetsuko Kuroyanagi, Japan's celebrity of television, films, and stage. She had invited David Hays and Linda to come to Japan in advance and appear on her TV show, *Tetsuko's Room*, the most popular program in Japan. Later, the NTD Company made its debut in the famed

Shinjuku Bunka Center of Tokyo before an SRO audience that included the Crown Prince, his wife and Prince Hitachi.

Tetsuko, Hays and Bove were presented to the Crown Prince and family during the intermission. The Crown Prince, who speaks English beautifully, later told the press that NTD's appearance was "one of his outstanding memories of the year and that it could be of great meaning to the deaf in the future in Japan."

It turned out to be a prophetic statement. Two years later, the deaf of Japan succeeded in establishing a professional theatre company along the lines of NTD. For Linda Bove and David Hays, the world tour helped fulfill another of NTD's objectives—the successful exchange of cultural experiences in the theatre arts between the deaf of America and those of foreign countries. In 1979, and for the next three years, Japan sent 10 representative deaf persons to study at the Summer School Program of the National Theatre of the Deaf, one of whom later became a member of the professional company.

Nor was Japan the only foreign country represented. Altogether, over 25 talented deaf foreigners have been invited to study with young deaf Americans at NTD's unique Summer Program—the Professional School for the Deaf Theatre Personnel and the only one of its kind in the world.

As a founding member of NTD, Linda Bove can take special pride in helping to "open doors" for other deaf performing artists to follow in her footsteps. And as a permanent member of *Sesame Street*, she is overjoyed at how deaf foreigners and native Americans build better bridges of understanding through the exciting experiences of cross-cultural communication in the theatre.

Michael Chatoff, one of a few deaf attorneys in America, was the first deaf lawyer to argue a case in front of the United States Supreme Court. This important event in the history of the deaf occurred on March 23, 1982. Chatoff, then 35 years old, represented a deaf girl, Amy Rowley, in a case which caught the attention of the entire nation.

At issue was whether administrators at the Furnace Woods Elementary School, where Amy was a student, had an obligation to provide an interpreter for her. Officials from the public school, located in Peekskill, New York, had argued unsuccessfully in District Court and the Circuit Court of Appeals that Amy didn't need an interpreter and that providing one was too expensive. Both times, the courts ruled in favor of the Rowleys and decreed that Amy receive interpreting services. Hoping for a reversal, the school district appealed to the U.S. Supreme Court.

Eventually, the highest court in the land agreed to hear the case. Thus, what started as a battle between a handful of school officials and a deaf girl's parents became something much bigger. Basically, the Court would be doing their own "interpreting"—defining what they believed to be the intent of the Education for All Handicapped Children Act of 1975 (Public Law 94-142). This federal law stipulated that handicapped students were entitled to a "free, appropriate education" and was a great step toward "equal opportunity" mainstreaming. But ever since the law was established, there was controversy over funding and the term "appropriate education." The Supreme Court now would decide exactly what was meant by the expression, and their final decision might have widespread impact—affecting handicapped students, and school districts, across the nation.

Michael Chatoff, who became deaf at the age of 22, had been the Rowleys' attorney from the beginning, representing the family and winning for them in the District and Circuit courts. He successfully argued that Amy's Individualized Education Program—which included an FM amplifier, a tutor for the deaf,

and a speech therapist—was not enough. Even with her excellent lip-reading ability, Chatoff contended, Amy could only understand 50% of classroom conversation. Accordingly, an interpreter as an additional support service was indispensible and most "appropriate" because Amy knew sign language well.

Chatoff himself used one kind of support service during both lower court hearings, employing a notetaker who recorded the courtroom drama. An interpreter wouldn't have helped much, since Chatoff was unskilled at sign language and lip-reading at the time. Although the notetaker was helpful and functioned as Chatoff's "ears," receiving quickly-scribbled notes left much to be desired. It was almost impossible for the notetaker to keep pace with the rapid give-and-take in the courtroom. But the method worked well enough to allow Chatoff to argue convincingly and win the cases.

The deaf lawyer hoped, however, to use a different system for the Supreme Court hearing. Rather than depend on notetaking, he envisioned using a computerized high-speed translation unit, known as Real Time Graphic Display. With this set-up, in which a stenotypist is used, Chatoff could read the justices' questions instantly on a video screen. The Real Time Graphic Display, which is being implemented at places like the National Technical Institute for the Deaf and by the National Captioning Institute, represents another achievement in technology for deaf consumers. In Chatoff's case, however, the only problem was that nothing like it had ever been brought into the Supreme Court, and he would need approval. In fact, no video devices of any kind—no cameras or monitors—were ever allowed within the Court's lofty walls.

Chatoff put in his request and then waited anxiously for the judges to make their decision. In the meantime, numerous attempts were made to try and dissuade him from participating. Alexander Stevas, the Court Clerk, sent a note to Chief Justice Warren Burger, stating that "Efforts to persuade [Chatoff] to have other counsel argue the case have not been fruitful." To the dismay of some, the dedicated deaf lawyer was determined to represent the Rowleys.

Just when he thought he would have to engage a notetaker again, the justices agreed to allow the equipment, thus enabling Chatoff to set two important precedents. Besides being the first deaf lawyer to argue before the U.S. Supreme Court, he was also one of the few attorneys to break the Court's entrenched traditions. Setting the latter precedent will hopefully help other deaf lawyers use the Graphic Display invention, if they so wish, in other courts.

What is the story behind this deaf man who chose to be the captain of his own ship, and whose determined voyage against the current of custom charted a new course for other deaf lawyers? Although he lost the decision by a very narrow margin, in which the Court ruled that Amy was doing well enough without the interpreter and that each school has the right to determine what is "appropriate" for a handicapped student, Chatoff's example of courage will not be forgotten. Even in losing, he made a giant stride for the deaf. In fact, he had already helped the deaf cause before he took the Rowley case.

Michael Chatoff was born in New York City on August 18, 1946. A true born-and-bred New Yorker, all of the schools and colleges he attended were in the "Big Apple." After attending Public Schools 173, 216 and Jamaica High, he enrolled in Queens College, graduating in 1967 with a B.A. and a Senate Service Award. From there, Chatoff went to Brooklyn Law School, receiving a J.D., Doctor of Law, degree in 1971. Seven years later, in 1978, he graduated from the New York University School of Law, earning a LL.M. degree.

It was while he was in the Brooklyn Law School that Chatoff lost his hearing. Two operations for bilateral acoustic neuroma, in which his tumorous auditory nerves were removed, left him totally deaf. But with the help of understanding professors and through his own tenacity, Chatoff was able to graduate from both schools.

After finishing at New York University, the future history-maker was employed in the Legal Department at the Chicago Title Insurance Company, in New York, until 1972. Since leaving there, he has worked for the West Publishing Company, in Mineola, New York, where he is senior legal editor in charge of the *United States Code Congressional and Administrative News.* This publication, which contains abstracts of recently enacted laws, informs the law community of the latest developments in the field.

While editing for West Publishing, Chatoff has been an active proponent of the deaf. He worked as a consultant to Senator Charles Mathias, writing a bill which Mathias introduced to Congress. The bill, known as *The Court Interpreters Act,* became law (P.L. 95-539) and was the Federal judicial system's first recognition of the special communications needs of the deaf.

In addition, Chatoff took the New York Telephone Company and the New York State Public Service Commission to court. He represented himself in the lawsuit *(Chatoff v. Public Service Commission),* citing that the phone company's rates discriminated against deaf people using TTYs for long distance phone calls. Communication by TTYs is much slower than by voice and more time consuming. Chatoff won the case and succeeded in getting a 25% rate reduction for deaf consumers of the telephone company's services. The ruling in that case helped set a precedent for similar rate reductions throughout the country.

Chatoff has also been active in the deaf community, serving as president of the New York Center for the Law and the Deaf; and as director of Westchester Community Services for the Hearing-Impaired. He has written many articles on the rights of the deaf, such as "A Tax Credit for the Deaf," and "The Deaf Individual in a Legal Setting."

Michael Chatoff's career in law and his service to the deaf are still in the early stages. Although he has given much, his legacy is incomplete. His valor and commitment to deaf equality, however, make it clear that the torch from Laurent Clerc has passed safely into worthy hands.

Kitty O'Neil, "Hollywood's most amazing stunt woman," has performed breath-taking feats in feature movies and television serials. She also set a world land speed record for a woman by zooming to 513 miles per hour in a three-wheeled rocket car. Yet, doing the impossible is nothing unusual for Kitty O'Neil, who has overcome handicaps all her life.

The daughter of a Cherokee Indian mother and Irish father, Kitty O'Neil was born on March 24, 1946 in Corpus Christi, Texas. While still an infant, she experienced her first set backs in life. Her father was killed in an airplane crash. At four months of age, she almost died when she contracted measles, mumps and scarlet fever. These three successive illnesses left her totally deaf and impaired her sense of balance.

Her mother, Patsy O'Neil, brought Kitty to live with her in Wichita Falls, Texas, where Kitty spent her first few years in almost total isolation. She could not communicate with others and there was nobody tó teach her how to read lips and talk. Her Indian mother decided to do something about that. She went to the University of Texas to study methods of teaching deaf children and obtained her certificate to teach. With great patience and skill, she taught Kitty to read lips and speak so that, at the age of eight, Kitty was prepared to enter the third grade in a regular public school. She surprised everyone by the good progress she made with hearing students.

Her mother encouraged Kitty to learn how to swim and dive so as to build up her strength and improve her sense of balance. She learned so well that, at the age of 14, she won the AAU Southwest District Junior Olympics diving championship in Texas.

When she was 16, Kitty moved to Anaheim, California to train with Dr. Sammy Lee, the two-time Olympic diving champion who ran a school for talented young divers. She also attended classes at Anaheim High School while putting in long hours of practice at Dr. Lee's diving school and competing in many events. By the age of 18, she had won five trophies and fifteen gold medals in high platform diving competition. She also graduated from Anaheim High with honors.

One year later, however, tragedy struck again. O'Neil became very ill with spinal meningitis and lay in bed for weeks. The doctors feared that she would never dive again, but they didn't know Kitty O'Neil. She set her mind to regaining her strength and skill, and two years later she won the women's 10 meter platform diving championship at the 1964 AAU Nationals.

Kitty went on to compete in the tryouts for the 1964 Olympic Games and she placed eighth in overall diving competition. She never won an Olympic medal, but she proved she could "comeback." She also had won enough awards during her career to fill up a show case—38 blue ribbons, 17 first place trophies, and 31 gold medals.

Always in search of new challenges, she next took an interest in speed racing on water. She went on to set two world speed records for women—racing in a high powered boat at 275.183 miles per hour and then hitting a high of 104.85 mph on water skis. She also raced snowmobiles, sand dune buggies, and motorcycles for the fun of it.

In 1970, while racing motorcycles in cross-country events, Kitty met Duffy Hambleton, a Hollywood stunt artist. Duffy taught her all the tricks of his profession, including survival techniques. In March, 1976, she successfully passed all tests and joined "Stunts Unlimited," an organization of the best daredevils.

Kitty became a "stand-in" for Hollywood and TV actresses whenever the scene was dangerous to human life. Her daredevil roles were many and they included substituting for Lee Grant who almost drowns in the sinking jet plane in *Airport '77*; for Lisa Blount when she is all ablaze with fire during a graveyard scene in the movie *9/30/55*; for Lana Wood when she is hanging out a window on the sixth floor in a TV episode of *Baretta*; for Lindsay Wagner when *The Bionic Woman* jumps off a speedboat; and for Linda Carter whenever *The Wonder*

Woman hurdles apartment rooftops or jumps from the 12th floor of a building.

Her most daring achievement occurred in December, 1976, when she was 28 years old. That is when Kitty O'Neil drove the "Motivator," a 48,000 horse-power rocket car which cost $350,000, over the Alvord Desert course in Fields, Oregon. Strapped down, in a position almost flat on her back, she clocked in at 512.710 miles per hour—a new land speed record for women which beat the old record by 200 mph! This amazing feat is now listed in the *Guiness Book of World Records.*

In 1978, O'Neil set two more records for women, driving from a "standing start." In a rocket-engined dragster, she accelerated to a speed of 392.5 miles per hour and an average speed of 178.9 mph over a quarter-mile course on El Mirage Dry Lake, California. This beat the previous records of 326 and 158 mph.

By 1981, Kitty O'Neil had set 26 world speed records on land. There were also two records as a stuntwoman—a 180 ft. high fall, and a 90 ft. high fall while on fire!

She has been featured as a "cover girl" on the front page of magazines and the story of her achievements has appeared in such leading publications as *The Saturday Evening Post, Readers Digest, Sports Illustrated,* and *The Women's Almanac.* In all these stories, Kitty has emphasized that she is not afraid of being deaf. Time and again she tells reporters: "I can do anything. I like to do things people say I can't do because I'm deaf. I have to work harder than some, but look at the fun I have proving they're wrong."

This is the message she often gets across to other deaf and handicapped people. She enjoys the opportunity to share the "deaf experience" with others, especially with children, and she always brightens up their day with her inspirational example. For being such an outstanding role model, the Alexander Graham Bell Association for the Deaf honored her with "The Volta Award" when she gave the keynote speech at their 1979 Convention.

In the same year, on February 25, 1979, her life story was featured as the CBS-TV Movie of the Week, entitled *Silent Victory: the Kitty O'Neil Story.* With movie star Stockard Channing in the leading role, the film dramatized the adventure-packed life of Kitty O'Neil and expressed her credo: "A handicap is not a defeat but a challenge to conquer." Naturally, Kitty herself performed all the daredevil stunts in the movie.

For a gal who stands 5 ft 3 inches and weighs 97 pounds, Kitty O'Neil is truly the *real life* "Wonder Woman"!

One of the biggest characters on television is Lou Ferrigno, best known as the star of the popular weekly program by CBS, *The Incredible Hulk.* As the "green giant" who crushed steel, broke through walls, and terrorized the meanest villains, Lou Ferrigno practically filled up the whole TV screen with his "Incredible Hulk"—a 6'5", 275 lb. titan with a 59" chest measurement and 23" biceps! What makes his story all the more incredible is the fact that Ferrigno was once a shy and skinny kid—just like the "90 lb. weakling" in the "Charles Atlas" advertisements.

Lou Ferrigno was born on November 9, 1951 and grew up in Brooklyn, New York. He suffered from an ear infection at the age of three, which resulted in a 75% permanent hearing loss. Because the hearing aids of the past weren't as advanced as today's, he developed a speech defect. This was harder to overcome than his hearing loss because people assumed he was "dumb" when they heard him talk. Lou's feelings of inferiority made him isolate himself from his schoolmates and avoid people.

For awhile, he attended a special educational program for the deaf at Public School 47, in Manhattan. Later, he transferred to a school in Brooklyn and took lessons in speech and lipreading on Saturdays. However, he still was misunderstood and called "dumb Louie" by the tough kids in his Brooklyn neighborhood.

One day, when he was 16 years old, the shy kid from Brooklyn who had let others tease him and "kick sand in his face" for so long, stepped into a local movie theatre. The feature was *Hercules,* starring Steve Reeves—and seeing it changed Louie's whole life. He decided to take up body building to try to change himself—like the kid in the "Charles Atlas" advertisement does—from a 90 lb. weakling into a mighty muscle man.

Louie began lifting weights in the basement of his home, and his mother thought he was crazy. When he was 19, he entered a "Mr. New Jersey" contest—and finished in 22nd place. Some people advised him to forget about body building.

But Lou refused to quit, and his father not only encouraged him but also became his trainer. Soon, the hard work began to pay off. Lou entered the AAU "Teenage Mr. America" competition and finished 4th. The same year, he won the "Teenage Mr. America" contest and a free trip to Switzerland.

The stage was now set for Ferrigno to test his muscles in big time competition. At the age of 20, he competed in the "Mr. Universe" contest as the underdog against 90 experienced opponents. He won by unanimous decision—the youngest ever to win the title! After that, he won the "Mr. Universe" title again, but lost the "Mr. Olympia" world class competition to another super body builder, the great Arnold Schwarzenegger. Both men are featured in the classic movie on body building, *Pumping Iron.*

Although he was winning trophies, the prize money was not enough for Ferrigno to earn a living. His first paying job was as a $10-an-hour sheet metal worker in a Brooklyn factory. He had learned the trade when he attended Brooklyn Technical High School. Although he stayed on the job for three years, he didn't enjoy the work, which was hard and dangerous. When a friend and co-worker accidentally cut off his hand one day, Ferrigno decided to look elsewhere for employment.

His first stop was in Canada, where he signed on as a defensive tackle for the Toronto "Argonauts" of the Canadian Football League. After playing in a couple of games, however, he injured his knee and left professional football. Down but not out, Ferrigno surfaced in Los Angeles in 1976 when he heard that Universal Studios was looking for a body-builder for the "Incredible Hulk" role. Lou auditioned and got the job.

Putting on "make up" for the Hulk required the former Mr. Universe to spend over two hours every day in cosmetic preparation. He was fitted with green contact lenses, a false scalp and wig. Then his body was sprayed with green paint. Needless to say, preparing for the role was almost as difficult as the role itself. The work was punishing, and Ferrigno even had to do his own stunts, which were sometimes dangerous. Once, he

MR· UNIVERSE AND THE HULK

jumped off a 30-foot-high wall. Another time, he was expected to run through a prop—a "wall" supposedly as flimsy as a fence made of toothpicks. A mistake had been made, however, and the wall was almost rock hard. When Ferrigno hit it while running at full speed, he bounced away like a ball. Even the green paint couldn't cover up some of his black and blue marks.

Like all television series must, *The Incredible Hulk* came to an end in 1981, after several very successful seasons. The series gave Ferrigno the experience he needed to pursue other roles, preferably speaking ones. He continued to take lessons in speech therapy to improve his speech, and one of his biggest boosters is his wife, Carla. They met in 1979 when she was working as a restaurant manager, and Lou found her to be very sensitive and understanding about his deafness and speech problems. They also found they share a common interest as Carla had previously worked with deaf children at the Neuropsychiatric Institute, University of California at Los Angeles.

In an interview for *People Magazine* (April, 1981), Lou Ferrigno stressed his determination to succeed as a speaking actor. He also joked that his wife, Carla "predicts I'll be the Clark Gable of the 80's"!

In recognition of his lifetime battle with his handicap, Ferrigno was chosen to serve as national chairman for *Better Speech and Hearing Month* (May, 1981), during its campaign to increase public awareness of the 22 million Americans with communicative disorders. For this, the National Technical Institute for the Deaf in Rochester, New York designed an eye-catching color poster which featured "strong man" Lou Ferrigno feeling the bicep muscles of cute little Sarah Halpert, a hearing impaired child. He was also honored by being named honorary director of the National Hearing Association "for his singular accomplishment in athletics and acting, and for his courageous example to all the hearing impaired youth of America that they, too, can be champions."

It's certain that Ferrigno will be setting more examples for both hearing-impaired and hearing youth everywhere in the coming years. In 1982, he was chosen for the starring role in a remake of the movie which inspired him as a youngster— *Hercules.* The fact that he was picked for the role, a speaking one, is a tribute to Lou Ferrigno's dedication, and recognition that he is not only a titan of body, but of spirit as well.

Bibliography

Books

Albronda, Mildred. *Douglas Tilden: Portrait of A Deaf Sculptor;* T.J. Publishers, Inc., Silver Spring, Md., 1980.

Athearn, Robert G. *War With Mexico, The American Heritage Illustrated History of the United States,* Vol. 7, Dell Publishing Co., N.Y., 1963.

Braddock, Guilbert C. *Notable Deaf Persons;* Florence B. Crammatte, ed. Gallaudet College Alumni Association, Washington, D.C., 1975.

Bray, Billy. *The Wonder Dancers: Woods and Bray* (Autobiography); Bray, Youngstown, Ohio, Third Edition, 1981.

Bruce, Robert V. *Alexander Graham Bell and the Conquest of Solitude;* Little, Brown and Company, Boston, 1973.

Burlingame, Roger. *Out of Silence Into Sound: The Life of Alexander Graham Bell;* The Macmillan Company, N.Y., 1964.

Choate, Anne and Helen Ferris (eds.). *Juliette Low and the Girl Scouts;* Doubleday Doran and Company, Inc., N.Y., 1928.

Davis, Mac. *100 Greatest Baseball Heroes;* Grossett and Dunlap, N.Y., 1974.

De Gering, Etta. *Gallaudet: Friend of the Deaf;* David McKay Company, N.Y., 1964.

Gannon, Jack R. *Deaf Heritage: A Narrative History of Deaf America;* National Association of the Deaf, Silver Spring, Md., 1981.

Huston, Cleburne. *Deaf Smith: Incredible Texas Spy;* Texian Press, Waco, Tex., 1974.

Hyde, George E. *Red Cloud's Folk: A History of the Ogala Sioux Indians,* [1957], University of Oklahoma Press, 1968.

Hyde, George E. *Spotted Tail's Folk: A History of the Brulé Sioux,* University of Oklahoma Press, 1961.

International Telephone Directory of the Deaf: 1976–1977. Teletypewriters for the Deaf, Inc., Washington, D.C., 1977.

Neft, David S., Richard M. Cohen and Jordan A. Deutsch. *The Complete All-Time Pro-Baseball Register;* Grossett and Dunlap, N.Y., 1979.

Our Heritage: Gallaudet College Centennial 1864–1964; Gallaudet College Alumni Association, D.C. Chapter, Graphic Arts Press, Washington, D.C., 1964.

Pace, Mildred M. *Juliette Low: Founder of the Girl Scouts;* Scribners, N.Y., 1947.

Panara, Robert F., Taras B. Denis and James H. McFarlane (eds.). *The Silent Muse: An Anthology of Poetry and Prose by the Deaf;* Gallaudet College Alumni Association, Toronto, Canada, 1960.

Powers, Helen. *Signs of Silence: Bernard Bragg and the National Theatre of the Deaf;* Dodd, Mead and Company, N.Y., 1972.

Reichler, Joseph L. *The Great All-Time Baseball Record Book;* Macmillan Company, Inc., N.Y., 1981.

Schein, Jerome D. *A Rose for Tomorrow: A Biography of Frederick C. Schreiber;* National Association of the Deaf, Silver Spring, Md., 1981.

Sesame Street. *Sign Language Fun with Linda Bove,* prepared in cooperation with the National Theatre of the Deaf, Random House/Children's Television Workshop, Random House Inc., N.Y., 1980.

Shultz, Gladys D. and Daisy Gordon Lawrence. *Lady from Savannah: The Life of Juliette Low*; J.B. Lippincott Company, Philadelphia, 1958.

Stensland, Anna Lee. *Literature by and About the American Indian: An Annotated Bibliography*, National Council of Teachers of English, Urbana, Ill., 1975.

Tidyman, Ernest. *Dummy*; Little, Brown and Company, Boston, 1974.

Unforgettable Characters. The Reader's Digest Editors; Berkley Books, N.Y., 1980.

Waite, Helen Elmira. *Make A Joyful Sound: The Romance of Mabel Hubbard and Alexander Graham Bell*; Macrae Smith Company, Philadelphia, 1961.

Woods, Willard H. *The Forgotten People*; Dixie Press, St. Petersburg, Fla., 1973.

Articles (Magazines, Journals, Newspapers)

"Andrew Jackson Foster Named Man of the year by the Alpha Sigma Pi Fraternity." *Public Relations News Release*, Gallaudet College, May 18, 1962.

Arnold, N. Hillis. "A Deaf Sculptor." *The Volta Review*, June, 1967.

"Art Kruger Receives Honorary Doctorate from Hofstra University." *The Silent News*, August, 1982.

Atkinson, Charlie. "Art Kruger: The Man Behind the U.S. Deaf Olympic Team." *The News Herald*, Morgantown, N.C., July 2, 1981.

"BBC-TV's 'The Legend of King Arthur' to be Close-Captioned in January." *The Silent News*, Nov. 1981.

Ballantyne, Dr. Donald. Personal history and memoirs, March 27, 1981.

Benderly, Beryl Lieff. "Bernard Bragg: A Lively Silence." *The Washington Post Magazine*, April 8, 1979.

Boatner, Edmund Burke. "Captioned Films for the Deaf." *The Deaf American*, Vol. 34, No. 6, 1982.

Boatner, Edmund Burke. "Thomas Scott Marr: A Biography." *The Nebraska Journal*, Vol. 65, No. 7, June 1936. Reprinted from the *American Era*.

Bowe, Frank, Jr. "Dr. Boyce R. Williams—Foremost in Rehabilitation of the Deaf." *The Deaf American*, June, 1973.

Bowe, Phil. "The Fastest Woman on Earth." *The Saturday Evening Post*, March, 1977.

Bragg, Bernard. "Bragg Visits 38 Cities on World Tour." *The Deaf American*, June, 1978.

Brown, Ruth. "Linda Bove: Sesame Street Star." *The Deaf American*, Dec. 1977.

"Captioned Films: An Up-to-date Report." *The Deaf American*, June, 1965.

Carney, Edward C. "A Great Leader Passes On." *The NAD Interstate*, No. 3, 1979.

Carr, Steven. "Bloomfielder, Dr. Ballantyne, Probes the Small World of Microsurgery." *Essex Journal*, Bloomfield, N.J., Aug. 23, 1979.

Chatoff, Michael A. Correspondence Interview, July 27 and September 3, 1982.

Chitwood, Donna. "Washburn: Gallaudet's Noted Artist-Correspondent." *Gallaudet Today*, Vol. 7, No. 2, Winter, 1976.

"Closed Captioning for the Hearing Impaired." *The Deaf American*, May, 1979.

Coats, G. Dewey. "The Two Glorious Lives of Laurent Clerc." *The Kentucky Standard*, Vol. 11, No. 12, Dec. 14, 1967. Reprinted from *The Missouri Record*.

"Deaf Child's Case Making History." *Times Union*, Rochester, N.Y., March 23, 1982.

"Deaf Lawyer Seeks Special 'Hearing'." *The Silent News*, March, 1982.

"Deaf Man Receives High Honor (Andrew Foster)." *The Silent News*, Oct. 1980. Reprinted from *The Christian News*, July–August, 1980.

"Deaf People Throughout the World Mourn Loss of Fred Schreiber." *The NAD Broadcaster*, Vol. 1, No. 4, September, 1979.

"Death Takes Famed Lifeguard." *The Deaf American*, Oct. 1974.

Degener, Patricia. "A Retrospective of Arnold Sculpture." *St. Louis Post-Dispatch*, May 1, 1983.

Denis, Taras B. "For Bernard Bragg, the World's A Stage." *The Deaf American*, October, 1977.

Domich, Harold J. "John Carlin: A Biographical Sketch." *American Annals of the Deaf*, Vol. 90, No. 4, September, 1945.

"Dr. Andrew Foster." *Gallaudet Today*, Vol. 5, No. 4, Summer, 1975.

"Dr. Norwood Speaks from Experience When the Topic is Captioning." *Caption*, National Captioning Institute, Summer, 1982.

"Dummy: CBS-TV Movie of the Week." *TV Guide*, May 26–June 1, 1979.

" 'Dummy' Lawyer Lowell Myers Takes Aim at Rights for the Deaf." *People Magazine*, May 21, 1979.

Ebert, Alan. "Phyllis Frelich: This Tony Winner's Silence Speaks Louder Than Words." *US Magazine*, August 5, 1980.

Elliott, George B. "The Art Kruger Story." *Program Book*, 15th Annual AAAD National Basketball Tournament, Atlanta, Ga., April, 1959.

"Eugene (Silent) Hairston." *The Ring*, The Ring Publishing Corp., N.Y., Vol. LXI, No. 6, July, 1982.

"Falling to the Occasion: Kitty O'Neil." *TV Guide*, Vol. 27, No. 8, February 24, 1979.

Ferrigno, Lou. "No Longer Silenced by Hearing Loss; the Hulk Debuts in A Speaking Role." *People Magazine*, April 10, 1981.

"Foster, Andrew Jackson Named Outstanding Alumnus at EMU." *Silent News*, December, 1980.

Gamble, Bob. "Bill Schyman—One of Us." *Sportorials*, International Association of Approved Basketball Officials, Vol. 29: 226, March, 1979.

Gilbert, Laura-Jean. "Backstage With Phyllis Frelich." *Gallaudet Today*, Vol. 11, No. 1, Fall, 1980.

Gilbert, Laura-Jean. "Linda Bove—At Work in the Medium." *Gallaudet Today*, Vol. 4, No. 2, Winter, 1973.

Gitlits, Ilya. "Theatre of the Deaf: An American 'Signs In'." *Soviet Life*, No. 2: 221, February, 1975.

Golladay, Loy E. (ed.). "Deaf Pilot Spans Continent in Own Piper Cub." *The American Era*, May–June, 1948.

Golladay, Loy E. "Laurent Clerc: America's Pioneer Deaf Teacher." *The Deaf American*, March, 1980.

Gough, John A. "Now See This: New Media Bring the Start of a New Era in Communication for the Deaf." *Audiovisual Instruction*, November, 1966.

"Hand Talk With Linda Bove." *Sesame Street Magazine*, May, 1978; December–January, 1978–79.

Harris, Mark Jonathan. "He Always Gives A Powerful Performance." *TV Guide*, Vol. 26, No. 48, December 2, 1978.

Hays, David. "We've Come of Age" (National Theatre of the Deaf). *Theatre Crafts*, January/February, 1969.

Hoag, Dr. Ralph L. "Federal Program Activities Providing Additional Educational and Employment Opportunities for the Deaf." *The Silent Worker*, July/August, 1964.

Humphreys, Robert R. "A New Era for Deaf Americans." *The Deaf American*, September, 1978.

Jackman, Frank. "Top Court Deaf to Sign-language Plea." *The Daily News*, N.Y., June 29, 1982.

Kakutani, Michiko. "Deaf Since Birth, Phyllis Frelich Became an Actress—and Now a Star." *The NAD Broadcaster*, May, 1980.

Kenamore, Jane A. (Archivist, Rosenberg Library, Galveston, Texas); "Le Roy Colombo." Newspaper articles and biographical data, September–November, 1979.

"Kitty O'Neil—It's Never Been Done Before." *New York*, April 26, 1982.

Kleiman, Dena. "Effect of Handicapped Ruling Unclear." *The New York Times*, June 29, 1982.

Kowalewski, Felix. "Hillis Arnold: American Deaf Sculptor." *The Deaf American*, November, 1972.

Kowalewski, Felix. "Profiles of Selected Deaf Artists." *Gallaudet Today*, Vol. 11, No. 4, Summer, 1981.

Kruger, Art. Correspondence and Vita, August 1, 1982.

Kruger, Art. "William E. Hoy: Pro Baseball Star." *The Silent Worker*, July, 1952.

"Kruger, Smith Honored." *NAD Broadcaster*, Vol. 4, No. 3, June, 1982.

"Linda Bove: Language of Love." *World Around You*, Vol. 1, No. 11, April 17, 1980.

"Lou Ferrigno: Discipline Is Important." *World Around You*, Vol. III, No. 4, October 15, 1981.

Mann, Jim. "Deaf Lawyer Wants to Make Case His Way." *Los Angeles Times*, March 23, 1982.

McDermott, John Dishon. "George E. Hyde." *Arizona and the West: A Quarterly Journal of History;* The University of Arizona Press, Vol. 17, 1975.

Milner, Louise B. "Dr. Donald Ballantyne—Deaf Researcher in Transplants." *The Deaf American*, November, 1965.

"NBS Captioning Device, the." *Gallaudet Today*, Vol. 4, No. 2, Winter, 1973.

Norwood, Malcolm J. Correspondence Interviews, December 14 and 21, 1982.

Panara, Robert F. "The Deaf American: Two Hundred Years of Progress." *NTID Focus*, October—November, 1976.

Panara, Robert F. "Deaf Studies in the English Curriculum." *The Deaf American*, April, 1974.

Panara, Robert F. "The Deaf Writer in America." *American Annals of the Deaf*, Part I and Part II, September and November, 1970.

Parezo, Stephen A. "Schyman Named Head Olympic Basketball Coach for the Deaf." *The News Leader*, Laurel, Md., November 20, 1980.

Peet, Elizabeth. "Our Hall of Fame." *Gallaudet College Alumni Bulletin*, Vol. 3, No. 6, June, 1952.

Phinizy, Coles. "A Rocket Ride to Glory and Gloom." *Sports Illustrated*, Vol. 46, No. 3, January 17, 1977.

Playbill. Longacre Theatre, June, 1980.

"R.I.T. and Better Hearing and Speech Month." *NTID Alumni News*, Rochester, N.Y., Summer, 1981.

Reynolds, Bill. "The Two Faces of Lou Ferrigno." *Muscle*, Builder Power Magazine, Vol. 41, No. 4, April, 1980.

"Robert Weitbrecht." *Gallaudet Today*, Vol. 4, No. 4, Summer, 1974.

Runde, Winfield Scott. "Douglas Tilden, Sculptor," *The Silent Worker*, December, 1952.

Scarlett, Harold. "Le Roy Colombo: Life Saver." *Houston Post*, May 8, 1966.

Schyman, Bill. Correspondence and Vita, September 1, 1982.

"Schyman: Standout De Paul Cager." *Chicago Sun-Times*, January 27, 1952.

Shaposka, Bert. "Boyce Williams: The VRA Investment in the Future of the American Deaf." *The Silent Worker*, May, 1964.

"Should Amy Get An Interpreter? The Supreme Court Will Decide." *World Around You*, Gallaudet College, April, 1982.

"Silent Hairston." *Ebony*, no date (ca. 1950).

"Silent Victory: The Kitty O'Neil Story." CBS-TV Movie of The Week, *TV Guide*, Vol. 27, No. 8, February 24, 1979.

Smith, Red. "Some of the Things Joe Reichler Knows." *The New York Times*, May 24, 1981.

"Sounds of Silence: Children of a Lesser God." *Newsweek*, April 14, 1980.

Swain, Robert L., Jr. "The Hero Who Gave His Name to Texas' Deaf Smith County." *The Deaf American*, December, 1969.

"Thomas Scott Marr." *Tennessee, The Volunteer State*, P.515f, Vol. 4, The Nashville Room, Public Library of Nashville, Tennessee, (no date).

"Tribute to A Friend in Sound and Sign: Dr. Boyce R. Williams." *Gallaudet Today*, Vol. 1, No. 2, Fall, 1970.

"Unlocking A Prisoner of Silence." *Time Magazine*, January 17, 1977.

Warshawsky, Leonard. "The Taylor-Made Story." *The Silent Worker*, September, 1952.

"White House Is the Scene of Presentation Ceremonies for Thomas Flight Award." *The Cavalier*, September 30, 1948.

"William Wolcott Beadell: Editor and Publisher." *The Observer*, Arlington, N.J. Special Commemorative Number, printed by the Employees of the *Arlington Observer*, July, 1931, from the Gallaudet College Library.

"William Wolcott Beadell." *The Iowa Hawkeye*, October 1, 1931, from the Gallaudet College Library.

Williams, Boyce R. Correspondence and Vita, October 8, 1982.

Williams, Boyce R. "Thirty-Three Years." *The Deaf American*, September, 1978.

Williams, Gurney III. "Lifesaving Surgery—Under A Lens." *Popular Mechanics*, March, 1979.

Yengich, Karen. "Schyman To Be Inducted in the AAAD Hall of Fame." *The News Leader*, Laurel, Md., March 29, 1979.

Videotaped Programs

Graybill, Patrick. "Interview With Phyllis Frelich." NTID-TV videotape, NTID-ITV, September 28, 1981.

Panara, Robert F. "Famous Deaf Americans," Part I and Part II, NTID-TV videotapes, NTID-ITV, June 3–5, 1982.

Panara, Robert F. "Interview With Bernard Bragg." NTID-TV videotape, NTID-ITV, May 8, 1978.

Panara, Robert F. "Interview With Dr. Donald Ballantyne." NTID-TV videotape, NTID-ITV, March 26, 1981.

Panara, Robert F. "Interview With Frances Woods." NTID-TV videotape, NTID-ITV, April 29, 1981.

Panara, Robert F. "Interview With Eugene 'Silent' Hairston." NTID-TV videotape, NTID-ITV, April 8, 1983.

ROBERT PANARA, Professor of English and Drama, was the first deaf person to join the professional staff of the National Technical Institute for the Deaf in 1967 when the program was initiated on the hearing college campus of Rochester (N.Y.) Institute of Technology. He attended Gallaudet College (B.A.); New York University (M.A.); and the Catholic University of America (doctoral studies). An educator of wide experience, he has taught at the New York School for the Deaf in White Plains (1945–49) and at Gallaudet College (1949–67). He has served as Faculty Fellow at the Summer School Program of the National Theatre of the Deaf (1967–83), as Visiting Professor at California State University, Northridge (1975–76) and has written numerous articles on methods of teaching the deaf and "Deaf Studies." Prof. Panara established the English Department and the Drama Club at NTID. As the first deaf professor to teach in the College of Liberal Arts at R.I.T., he also developed several popular courses in "Deaf Studies" and helped pioneer the movement in America. A talented poet, he was the first recipient of the "Teegarden Award for Creative Poetry" at Gallaudet College (1945) and co-edited *The Silent Muse Anthology of Prose and Poetry by the Deaf* (1960). Among his citations are the "Outstanding Teaching Award" from R.I.T. (1974); the "National Award of Merit" from the World Federation of the Deaf (1975); and the "Humanitarian Award in Theatre of the Deaf" from Gallaudet College in 1977.

JOHN PANARA, a Captioning Specialist at the National Technical Institute for the Deaf, spends part of his time side-stepping the immense shadow cast by his famous father, but, like most left-handers, has learned to adapt well to any situation. His student years were spent at the State University of New York, College at Brockport, where he received a bachelor's degree and M.A. degree in English. He first joined NTID in 1977 as a Research and Training Assistant in the Department of Support Services, helping develop NTID's Tutor/Notetaker Training Program. He has been involved in numerous regional and national workshops on support services and is co-author of *The Tutor/ Notetaker Manager's Guide*, a resource manual for educators providing support services to mainstreamed secondary and post-secondary hearing-impaired students. In addition to working as a captioner in the Instructional Television Department, he teaches "Literature" and "Deaf Heritage" courses, and tutors students in NTID's English Learning Center.

KEVIN MULHOLLAND, an illustrator and graduate of the Rochester Institute of Technology, was born in New York City. After graduating from the New York School for the Deaf in White Plains, N.Y., he was employed as an illustrator by the Nestle Company of White Plains, N.Y., for 20 years. He studied illustration and TV art media at the Visual Arts School of New York City during evenings. In 1974, he enrolled in the National Technical Institute for the Deaf, receiving an A.A.S. degree in Visual Communications, and then obtained the B.S. degree in A-V Communications from the College of Applied Science and Technology, R.I.T. He has held teaching positions in the graphic arts at the New York School for the Deaf and the Louisiana School for the Deaf. He currently lives in Northridge, California, where he is involved in a new project as a book illustrator. He expects to pursue graduate studies leading to a Master's degree in Deaf Education so as to teach deaf and hearing students at the high school and college level.